TEX-MEX RECIPES

Publications International, Ltd.

Favorite Brand Name Recipes at www.fbnr.com

Pictured on the front cover: Southwestern Corn and Beans *(page 136).*

Pictured on the back cover *(clockwise from top left):* Fiesta Beef Enchiladas *(page 60),* Three-Bean Mole Chili *(page 56),* Mexican Sugar Cookies (Polvorones) *(page 149)* and Fiery Chili Beef *(page 104).*

Illustrated by Anne Crosse.

ISBN-13: 978-1-4127-2259-9
ISBN-10: 1-4127-2259-4

Library of Congress Control Number: 2005926113

Manufactured in China.

8 7 6 5 4 3 2 1

Microwave Cooking: Microwave ovens vary in wattage. Use the cooking times as guidelines and check for doneness before adding more time.

Preparation/Cooking Times: Preparation times are based on the approximate amount of time required to assemble the recipe before cooking, baking, chilling or serving. These times include preparation steps such as measuring, chopping and mixing. The fact that some preparations and cooking can be done simultaneously is taken into account. Preparation of optional ingredients and serving suggestions is not included.

Contents

Tejano Starters

Easy Taco Dip

½ pound ground beef chuck
1 cup frozen corn
½ cup chopped onion
½ cup salsa
½ cup mild taco sauce
1 can (4 ounces) diced mild green chilies
1 can (4 ounces) sliced ripe olives, drained
1 cup (4 ounces) shredded Mexican cheese blend
Tortilla chips
Sour cream

SLOW COOKER DIRECTIONS

1. Brown ground beef in large nonstick skillet over medium-high heat, stirring to separate meat. Drain and discard fat. Spoon into slow cooker.

2. Add corn, onion, salsa, taco sauce, chilies and olives to slow cooker; mix well. Cover; cook on LOW 2 to 4 hours.

3. Just before serving, stir in cheese. Serve with tortilla chips and sour cream.   *Makes about 3 cups dip*

TIP: To keep this dip hot through an entire party, simply leave it in the slow cooker on LOW.

PREP TIME: 15 minutes
COOK TIME: 2 to 4 hours

EASY TACO DIP

4

Hearty Nachos

1 pound ground beef
1 envelope LIPTON® RECIPE SECRETS® Onion Soup Mix
1 can (19 ounces) black beans, rinsed and drained
1 cup prepared salsa
1 package (8½ ounces) plain tortilla chips
1 cup shredded Cheddar cheese (about 4 ounces)

1. In 12-inch nonstick skillet, brown ground beef over medium-high heat; drain.

2. Stir in soup mix, black beans and salsa. Bring to a boil over high heat. Reduce heat to low and simmer 5 minutes or until heated through.

3. Arrange tortilla chips on serving platter. Spread beef mixture over chips; sprinkle with Cheddar cheese. Top, if desired, with sliced green onions, sliced pitted ripe olives, chopped tomato and chopped cilantro.   *Makes 8 servings*

PREP TIME: 10 minutes
COOK TIME: 12 minutes

SOUTHWESTERN QUESADILLAS

3 (8-inch) flour tortillas
    I CAN'T BELIEVE IT'S NOT BUTTER!® Spray
¼ teaspoon chili powder, divided
⅛ teaspoon ground cumin, divided
1 cup shredded Monterey Jack or cheddar cheese
    (about 4 ounces)
1 can (4 ounces) chopped green chilies, drained
1 can (2¼ ounces) sliced pitted ripe olives, drained
2 tablespoons chopped cilantro (optional)

Generously spray one side of one tortilla with I Can't Believe It's Not Butter!® Spray. Sprinkle with ½ of the chili powder and cumin. On baking sheet, arrange tortilla spice-side down, then top with ½ of the cheese, chilies, olives and cilantro. Top with second tortilla. Repeat layers, ending with tortilla. Spray top tortilla generously with I Can't Believe It's Not Butter!® Spray, then sprinkle with remaining chili powder and cumin. Grill or broil until tortillas are golden and cheese is melted. Cut in wedges and serve, if desired, with salsa.   *Makes 4 servings*

SOUTHWESTERN QUESADILLAS

SANGRIA COMPOTE

½ cup sugar
½ cup water
1 cinnamon stick
3 whole cloves
⅛ teaspoon ground nutmeg
2 (1-inch-wide) strips orange peel
2 (1-inch-wide) strips lemon peel
6 cups assorted fruits and berries: sliced, peeled fresh or unsweetened frozen peaches; pitted Bing cherries; blueberries; small, hulled strawberries; red and green seedless grapes; cantaloupe and honeydew melon balls; peeled, cored and diced pears
1 cup dry red wine or rose wine
¼ cup orange juice
1 teaspoon lemon juice
   Mint sprigs for garnish

1. Combine sugar, water, cinnamon stick, cloves, nutmeg, orange peel and lemon peel in small saucepan. Cook, stirring occasionally, over medium heat until sugar is dissolved. Cover; reduce heat and simmer 5 minutes. Let cool.

2. Place fruits and berries in large bowl. Pour sugar mixture through strainer over fruit. Discard spices and peels. Add wine, orange juice and lemon juice. Stir gently to mix. Cover and refrigerate 1 hour or up to 2 days for flavors to blend.

3. To serve, spoon about ¾ cup fruit into each of 8 bowls. Pour about ¼ cup wine mixture over each serving. Garnish with mint sprigs.   *Makes 8 servings*

7-LAYER SOMBRERO DIP

    1 can (16 ounces) refried beans
    1 container (8 ounces) sour cream (1 cup)
    1 packet (1 ounce) HIDDEN VALLEY® The Original
        Ranch® Dips Mix
    1 cup diced tomatoes
    1 can (4 ounces) diced green chiles, rinsed and drained
    1 can (2¼ ounces) sliced ripe olives, rinsed and drained
    ¾ cup (3 ounces) shredded Cheddar cheese
    ¾ cup (3 ounces) shredded Monterey Jack cheese
        Chopped avocado (optional)
        Tortilla chips, for dipping

Spread beans on a 10-inch serving platter. Blend sour cream
and dips mix. Spread over beans. Layer tomatoes, chiles,
olives, Cheddar cheese, Monterey Jack cheese and avocado,
if desired. Serve with tortilla chips.   *Makes 8 to 10 servings*

FIERY BEAN DIP

    1 can (16 ounces) refried beans
    1 package (8 ounces) pasteurized process cheese, cubed
    ½ cup mild chunky salsa
    ⅓ cup *Frank's® RedHot®* Original Cayenne Pepper Sauce
        Tortilla chips
        Vegetable dippers

1. Combine beans, cheese, salsa and *Frank's RedHot* Sauce in
large saucepan. Cook and stir over medium heat 5 minutes or
until cheese melts and mixture is well blended.

2. Serve with tortilla chips or vegetable dippers.
                                        Makes 3 cups dip

PREP TIME: 5 minutes
COOK TIME: 5 minutes

TEX-MEX POTATO SKINS

3 hot baked potatoes, split lengthwise
¾ cup (3 ounces) shredded Cheddar or pepper Jack cheese
1⅓ cups *French's®* French Fried Onions, divided
¼ cup chopped green chilies
¼ cup cooked crumbled bacon
Salsa and sour cream

1. Preheat oven to 350°F. Scoop out inside of potatoes leaving ¼-inch shells. Reserve inside of potatoes for another use.

2. Arrange potato halves on baking sheet. Top with cheese, ⅔ *cup* French Fried Onions, chilies and bacon.

3. Bake 15 minutes or until heated through and cheese is melted. Cut each potato half crosswise into thirds. Serve topped with salsa, sour cream and remaining onions.

Makes 18 appetizer servings

VARIATION: For added Cheddar flavor, substitute *French's®* **Cheddar French Fried Onions** for the original flavor.

FRESH TOMATO SALSA

1 medium tomato, finely chopped
¼ cup coarsely chopped fresh cilantro
2 tablespoons finely chopped white onion
1 fresh jalapeño pepper,* seeded, finely chopped
1 tablespoon fresh lime juice

*Jalapeño peppers can sting and irritate the skin; wear rubber gloves when handling peppers and do not touch eyes. Wash hands after handling peppers.

Combine all ingredients in small bowl; mix well. Let stand, covered, at room temperature 1 to 2 hours to blend flavors.

Makes about ¾ cup

TEX-MEX POTATO SKINS

EASY SAUSAGE EMPANADAS

¼ pound bulk pork sausage
1 (15-ounce) package refrigerated pie crusts (2 crusts)
2 tablespoons finely chopped onion
⅛ teaspoon garlic powder
⅛ teaspoon ground cumin
⅛ teaspoon dried oregano, crushed
1 tablespoon chopped pimiento-stuffed olives
1 tablespoon chopped raisins
1 egg, separated

Let pie crusts stand at room temperature for 20 minutes or according to package directions. Crumble sausage into medium skillet. Add onion, garlic powder, cumin and oregano; cook over medium-high heat until sausage is no longer pink. Drain drippings. Stir in olives and raisins. Beat egg yolk slightly; stir into sausage mixture, mixing well. Carefully unfold crusts. Cut into desired shapes using 3-inch cookie cutters. Place about 2 teaspoons sausage filling on half the cutouts. Top with remaining cutouts. (Or, use round cutter, top with sausage filling and fold dough over to create half-moon shape.) Moisten fingers with water and pinch dough to seal edges. Slightly beat egg white; gently brush over tops of empanadas. Bake in 425°F oven 15 to 18 minutes or until golden brown.   *Makes 12 appetizer servings*

PREP TIME: 25 minutes
COOK TIME: 15 minutes

Favorite recipe from **National Pork Board**

EASY SAUSAGE EMPANADAS

Tex-Mex Hot Dip

1 pound BOB EVANS® Original Recipe Roll Sausage
½ cup chopped onion
⅓ cup chopped bell pepper (red, yellow or green)
½ cup diced fresh tomato
¼ cup chopped fresh cilantro
1 (4-ounce) can chili peppers, drained and chopped
1 teaspoon hot pepper sauce
½ teaspoon ground cumin
½ teaspoon chili powder
2 cups (8 ounces) shredded Monterey Jack cheese
2 cups (8 ounces) shredded Cheddar cheese
1 (14-ounce) bag corn tortilla chips

Preheat oven to 350°F. Cook sausage, onion and bell pepper in large skillet until sausage is browned; drain on paper towels. Place in 2-quart casserole dish. Stir in tomato, cilantro, chili peppers, hot pepper sauce, cumin and chili powder. Top with cheeses; bake, uncovered, 10 to 15 minutes or until dip is heated through and cheese is melted. Serve with tortilla chips. Refrigerate leftovers. *Makes 10 to 12 servings*

HOT CHEESY CHILI DIP

    1 pound lean ground beef
    ½ cup chopped onion
    1 package (1 pound) pasteurized process cheese spread
        with jalapeño pepper, cut into cubes
    1 can (15 ounces) kidney beans, drained
    1 bottle (12 ounces) HEINZ® Chili Sauce
    ¼ cup chopped fresh parsley
        Tortilla chips or crackers

In large saucepan, cook beef and onion until onion is tender;
drain. Stir in cheese, beans and chili sauce; heat, stirring until
cheese is melted. Stir in parsley. Serve warm with tortilla chips
or crackers.   *Makes about 5 cups*

GREEN CHILI SALSA

    1 can (14½ ounces) diced tomatoes, drained
    1 can (4 ounces) diced green chilies, drained
    ½ cup chopped green onions with tops
    2 tablespoons chopped fresh cilantro
    1 fresh jalapeño or serrano pepper,* stemmed, seeded
        and minced
    1 tablespoon lime juice
    1 teaspoon vegetable oil
    1 clove garlic, minced
        Salt

*Jalapeño and serrano peppers can sting and irritate the skin; wear rubber gloves
when handling peppers and do not touch eyes. Wash hands after handling.

Combine tomatoes, green chilies, onions, cilantro, jalapeño,
lime juice, oil and garlic in medium bowl. Add salt to taste.
Cover; refrigerate 1 hour or up to 3 days for flavors to blend.
                                                Makes about 2 cups

Tejano Starters 17

RIO GRANDE SALSA

1 tablespoon vegetable oil
1 onion, chopped
3 cloves garlic, minced
2 teaspoons ground cumin
1½ teaspoons chili powder
2 cans (14½ ounces each) diced tomatoes, drained
1 canned chipotle chili pepper, seeded and finely diced
1 teaspoon adobo sauce from canned chili pepper
½ cup chopped fresh cilantro
¾ teaspoon sugar
½ teaspoon salt

1. Heat oil in medium saucepan over medium-high heat until hot. Add onion and garlic. Cook and stir 5 minutes or until onion is tender. Add cumin and chili powder; cook 30 seconds, stirring frequently. Add tomatoes, chili pepper and adobo sauce. Reduce heat to medium-low. Simmer 10 to 12 minutes or until salsa is thickened, stirring occasionally.

2. Remove saucepan from heat; stir in cilantro, sugar and salt. Cool completely. Serve or store in airtight container in refrigerator up to 3 weeks. *Makes about 3 cups*

NOTE: This salsa is very spicy. For a milder version, use only 1 teaspoon finely diced chipotle chili pepper.

RIO GRANDE SALSA

GRILLED QUESADILLA SNACKS

1½ cups (6 ounces) shredded Monterey Jack cheese
½ red or yellow bell pepper, chopped
2 ounces sliced smoked ham, cut into thin strips
2 ounces sliced smoked turkey, cut into thin strips
¼ cup finely chopped green onions
⅓ cup *French's*® Classic Yellow® Mustard
2 teaspoons ground cumin
10 flour tortillas (6 inch)

1. Combine cheese, bell pepper, ham, turkey and onions in medium bowl. Combine mustard and cumin in small bowl; mix well.

2. Place 5 tortillas on sheet of waxed paper. Spread 1 rounded teaspoon mustard mixture over each tortilla. Sprinkle cheese mixture evenly over mustard mixture. Top with another tortilla, pressing down firmly to form quesadilla.

3. Place quesadillas on oiled grid. Grill over medium heat 2 minutes or until cheese is melted and quesadillas are heated through, turning once. Cut each quesadilla into quarters. Serve with salsa and cilantro, if desired.   *Makes 10 servings*

PREP TIME: 30 minutes
COOK TIME: 2 minutes

tip Whether served as a snack or a meal, quesadillas are exceptionally easy to make. Simply stuff your favorite filling (shredded cheese, sautéed vegetables or chopped cooked meats) into a flour or corn tortilla. Fold over to make a "turnover" or top with another tortilla. Either toast on the grill or in a skillet until the cheese is melted and tortillas are golden brown.

GRILLED QUESADILLA SNACKS

CHEESY CHORIZO WEDGES

Red & Green Salsa (page 23)
8 ounces chorizo
1 cup (4 ounces) shredded mild Cheddar cheese
1 cup (4 ounces) shredded Monterey Jack cheese
3 flour tortillas (10-inch diameter)

1. Prepare Red & Green Salsa.

2. Remove and discard casing from chorizo. Heat medium skillet over high heat until hot. Reduce heat to medium. Crumble chorizo into skillet. Brown 6 to 8 minutes, stirring to separate meat. Remove with slotted spoon; drain on paper towels.

3. Preheat oven to 450°F. Combine cheeses in small bowl.

4. Place tortillas on baking sheets. Divide chorizo evenly among tortillas, leaving ½ inch of edges of tortillas uncovered. Sprinkle cheese mixture over top.

5. Bake 8 to 10 minutes until edges are crisp and golden and cheese is bubbly and melted.

6. Transfer to serving plates; cut each tortilla into 6 wedges. Serve with Red & Green Salsa. *Makes 6 to 8 servings*

Red & Green Salsa

- 1 small red bell pepper
- ¼ cup coarsely chopped fresh cilantro
- 3 green onions, cut into thin slices
- 2 fresh jalapeño peppers,* seeded, minced
- 2 tablespoons fresh lime juice
- 1 clove garlic, minced
- ¼ teaspoon salt

*Jalapeño peppers can sting and irritate the skin; wear rubber gloves when handling peppers and do not touch eyes. Wash hands after handling.

1. Cut bell pepper lengthwise in half; remove and discard seeds and veins. Cut halves lengthwise into thin slivers; cut slivers crosswise into halves.

2. Mix all ingredients in small bowl. Let stand, covered, at room temperature 1 to 2 hours to blend flavors.

Makes 1 cup

Zesty Pico de Gallo

- 2 cups chopped, seeded tomatoes
- 1 cup chopped green onions
- 1 can (8 ounces) tomato sauce
- ½ cup minced fresh cilantro
- 1 to 2 tablespoons minced jalapeño peppers*
- 1 tablespoon fresh lime juice

*Jalapeño peppers can sting and irritate the skin; wear rubber gloves when handling peppers and do not touch eyes. Wash hands after handling.

Combine all ingredients in medium bowl. Cover and refrigerate at least 1 hour.

Makes 4 cups

CHILI CON QUESO

2 tablespoons butter
¼ cup finely chopped onion
1 clove garlic, minced
1 can (8 ounces) tomato sauce
1 can (4 ounces) diced green chilies, drained
2 cups (8 ounces) shredded Cheddar cheese
2 cups (8 ounces) shredded Monterey Jack cheese
   with jalapeño peppers
  Tortilla chips and crisp raw vegetable dippers

1. Melt butter in 3- to 4-quart saucepan over medium heat. Add onion and garlic; cook until onion is tender. Stir in tomato sauce and chilies; reduce heat to low. Simmer 3 minutes. Gradually add cheeses; stir until cheeses are melted and mixture is evenly blended.

2. Transfer to fondue pot or chafing dish; keep warm over heat source. Serve with tortilla chips and vegetable dippers.

Makes 3 cups (about 12 servings)

MAKE-AHEAD SOUTHWESTERN CHILI CHEESE EMPANADAS

¾ cup (3 ounces) finely shredded taco-flavored cheese*
⅓ cup diced green chilies, drained
1 package (15 ounces) refrigerated pie crusts
1 egg
  Chili powder

*If taco-flavored cheese is unavailable, toss ¾ cup shredded Monterey Jack cheese with ½ teaspoon chili powder.

1. Combine cheese and chilies in small bowl.

2. Unfold 1 pastry crust on floured surface. Roll into 13-inch circle. Cut dough into 16 rounds using 3-inch cookie cutter, rerolling scraps as necessary. Repeat with remaining crust to make 32 circles.

3. Spoon 1 teaspoon cheese mixture in center of each dough round. Fold round in half, sealing edge with tines of fork.

4. Place empanadas on wax paper-lined baking sheets; freeze, uncovered, 1 hour or until firm. Place in resealable plastic food storage bags. Freeze up to 2 months, if desired.

5. To complete recipe, preheat oven to 400°F. Place frozen empanadas on ungreased baking sheet. Beat egg and 1 tablespoon water in small bowl; brush on empanadas. Sprinkle with chili powder.

6. Bake 12 to 17 minutes or until golden brown. Remove from baking sheet to wire rack to cool.   *Makes 32 appetizers*

SERVING SUGGESTION: Serve empanadas with salsa.

MAKE-AHEAD TIME: up to 2 months in freezer
FINAL PREP TIME: 30 minutes

SANGRITA

 3 cups DEL MONTE® Tomato Juice
1½ cups orange juice
 ½ cup salsa
 Juice of 1 medium lime

1. Mix all ingredients in large pitcher; chill.

2. Serve over ice with fruit garnishes, if desired.

Makes 6 (6-ounce) servings

PREP TIME: 3 minutes

TEX-MEX ARTICHOKE DIP

 1 cup *French's® Gourmayo™* Smoked Chipotle Light
    Mayonnaise
 ½ cup sour cream
 1 can (14 ounces) artichoke hearts, drained well and
    chopped
 ¾ cup shredded Monterey Jack cheese
 ¼ cup chopped roasted red pepper
 2 green onions, chopped

1. Preheat oven to 375°F. In large bowl, combine mayonnaise and sour cream. Stir in artichokes, cheese, red pepper and green onions. Spoon into 9-inch pie plate or 1-quart shallow baking dish.

2. Bake for 30 minutes or until hot. Stir well before serving. Serve with assorted crackers and cut-up vegetables.

Makes 13 (¼-cup) servings

PREP TIME: 10 minutes
COOK TIME: 30 minutes

MARGARITAS

  8 ounces tequila
  4 ounces Triple Sec
  8 ounces fresh lime juice
  ¼ cup sugar
    Crushed ice
    Additional lime juice (for glass rims, optional)
    Coarse or kosher salt (for glass rims, optional)

In blender jar, mix tequila, Triple Sec, lime juice, sugar and crushed ice until frothy. Dip rim of glass in lime juice, then in salt, if desired. Fill with margarita mixture.

Makes 4 servings

SERVING SUGGESTION: Serve in an iced pitcher with all your favorite Mexican entrées or appetizers. Great for parties.

VARIATIONS: May use about 8 ounces sweet-and-sour bar mix in place of fresh lime juice and sugar. To make Strawberry Margaritas, blend in about 1 to 1½ cups fresh strawberries.

PREP TIME: 10 to 15 minutes.

Favorite recipe from Lawrys® Foods

TACO DIP

   12 ounces cream cheese, softened
   ½ cup sour cream
   2 teaspoons chili powder
1½ teaspoons ground cumin
   ⅛ teaspoon ground red pepper
   ½ cup salsa
      Crisp salad greens
   1 cup (4 ounces) shredded Cheddar cheese
   1 cup (4 ounces) shredded Monterey Jack cheese
   ½ cup diced plum tomatoes
   ⅓ cup sliced green onions
   ¼ cup sliced pitted ripe olives
   ¼ cup sliced pimiento-stuffed green olives
      Tortilla chips and blue corn chips

1. Combine cream cheese, sour cream, chili powder, cumin and ground red pepper in large bowl; mix until well blended. Stir in salsa.

2. Spread dip onto greens-lined serving platter.

3. Top with cheeses, tomatoes, green onions, ripe olives and green olives.

4. Serve with chips.   *Makes 10 servings*

TACO DIP

SPICY VEGETABLE QUESADILLAS

   1 small zucchini, chopped
   ½ cup chopped green bell pepper
   ½ cup chopped onion
   2 cloves garlic, minced
   ½ teaspoon chili powder
   ½ teaspoon ground cumin
   8 (6-inch) flour tortillas
   1 cup (4 ounces) shredded Cheddar cheese
   ¼ cup chopped fresh cilantro

1. Spray large nonstick skillet with nonstick cooking spray. Heat over medium heat until hot. Add zucchini, pepper, onion, garlic, chili powder and cumin; cook and stir 3 to 4 minutes or until vegetables are crisp-tender. Remove vegetables and set aside; wipe skillet clean.

2. Spoon vegetable mixture evenly over half of each tortilla. Sprinkle each evenly with cheese and cilantro. Fold each tortilla in half.

3. Spray same skillet with cooking spray. Add tortillas and heat 1 to 2 minutes per side over medium heat or until lightly browned. Cut into thirds before serving.   *Makes 8 servings*

tip Make countless new flavor combinations for these quesadillas by substituting different types of shredded cheeses such as Monterey Jack, queso Chihuahua, Pepper Jack or smoked Gouda for the Cheddar cheese.

TEX-MEX GUACAMOLE PLATTER

    4 ripe avocados
    ¼ cup lime juice
    3 large cloves garlic, crushed
    2 tablespoons olive oil
    ½ teaspoon salt
    ¼ teaspoon black pepper
    1 cup (4 ounces) shredded Colby-Jack cheese
    1 cup seeded, diced plum tomatoes
    ⅓ cup sliced and pitted ripe olives
    ⅓ cup prepared salsa
    1 tablespoon minced fresh cilantro
      Tortilla chips

1. Cut avocados in half, remove pits and scoop out flesh into food processor. Add lime juice, garlic, olive oil, salt and pepper. Process until almost smooth.

2. Spread avocado mixture evenly on large dinner plate or serving platter, leaving a border around edge. Top with cheese, tomatoes, olives, salsa and cilantro. Serve with chips.

Makes 6 to 8 servings

tip To satisfy that craving for guacamole, either speed up ripening the avocados in the microwave or purchase frozen peeled and seeded avocados. To soften an underripe avocado (which has been brought to room temperature), microwave at HIGH 30 to 40 seconds or just until soft. Allow to cool before using. Or, simply defrost frozen avocados and proceed with the recipe.

TEX-MEX GUACAMOLE PLATTER

Chilis, Soups & Breads

QUICK CORN BREAD WITH CHILIES 'N' CHEESE

- 1 package (12 to 16 ounces) corn bread or corn muffin mix
- 1 cup (4 ounces) shredded Monterey Jack cheese, divided
- 1 can (4 ounces) chopped green chilies, drained
- 1 envelope LIPTON® RECIPE SECRETS® Vegetable Soup Mix

Prepare corn bread mix according to package directions; stir in ½ cup cheese, chilies and vegetable soup mix. Pour batter into lightly greased 8-inch baking pan; bake as directed. While warm, top with remaining ½ cup cheese. Cool completely on wire rack. To serve, cut into squares. *Makes 16 servings*

QUICK CORN BREAD WITH CHILIES 'N' CHEESE

EASY CHILE VERDE

     2 teaspoons vegetable oil
1½ pounds lean, boneless pork, cut into thin strips
     1 large onion, halved and thinly sliced
     1 can (14.5 ounces) diced tomatoes with juice
     1 can (7 ounces) diced green chiles
     2 packages (0.88 ounce each) LAWRY'S® Brown
          Gravy Mix
  ¾ cup water

In large skillet, heat oil over high heat; brown pork and
onions. Add remaining ingredients; mix thoroughly. Bring
to a boil; reduce heat to low and cook 20 to 25 minutes or
until meat is tender and thoroughly cooked. Stir occasionally.

Makes 6 servings

MEAL IDEA: Serve over cooked rice or wrap up in warmed
tortillas. Fresh fruit or green salad add the final touch to the
meal!

SERVING SUGGESTIONS: Serve as a filling for burritos or great
over baked potatoes.

PREP TIME: 10 minutes
COOK TIME: 30 to 35 minutes

Salsa Corn Soup with Chicken

- 3 quarts chicken broth
- 2 pounds boneless skinless chicken breasts, cooked and diced
- 2 packages (10 ounces each) frozen whole kernel corn, thawed
- 4 jars (11 ounces each) NEWMAN'S OWN® All Natural Salsa
- 4 large carrots, diced

Bring chicken broth to a boil in Dutch oven. Add chicken, corn, Newman's Own® Salsa and carrots. Bring to a boil. Reduce heat and simmer until carrots are tender.

Makes 8 servings

tip Serve a wedge of lime with each bowl of soup. The lime not only serves as a colorful garnish but perks up the flavor when the lime juice is squirted in the soup.

Chilis, Soups & Breads ⟨ *39* ⟩

TEX-MEX CHICKEN & RICE CHILI

  1 package (6.8 ounces) RICE-A-RONI® Spanish Rice

2¾ cups water

  2 cups chopped cooked chicken or turkey

  1 can (15 or 16 ounces) kidney beans or pinto beans, rinsed and drained

  1 can (14½ or 16 ounces) tomatoes or stewed tomatoes, undrained

  1 medium green bell pepper, cut into ½-inch pieces

1½ teaspoons chili powder

  1 teaspoon ground cumin

  ½ cup (2 ounces) shredded Cheddar or Monterey Jack cheese (optional)

    Sour cream (optional)

    Chopped cilantro (optional)

1. In 3-quart saucepan, combine rice-vermicelli mix, Special Seasonings, water, chicken, beans, tomatoes, green pepper, chili powder and cumin. Bring to a boil over high heat.

2. Reduce heat to low; simmer, uncovered, about 20 minutes or until rice is tender, stirring occasionally.

3. Top with cheese, sour cream and cilantro, if desired.

Makes 4 servings

TEX-MEX CHICKEN & RICE CHILI

SPICY CORNBREAD

1 pound BOB EVANS® Original Recipe Roll Sausage
3 green onions with tops, chopped
1½ cups biscuit mix
1 cup cornmeal
1 cup grated longhorn cheese
⅔ cup milk
½ cup thick and chunky picante sauce
1 egg, lightly beaten
2 teaspoons hot pepper sauce, or to taste
1 jalapeño pepper, seeded and chopped (optional)

Preheat oven to 400°F. Crumble sausage into large skillet. Add onions. Cook over medium heat until sausage is browned, stirring occasionally. Drain off any drippings. Place sausage mixture in large bowl; add remaining ingredients, mixing well with wooden spoon. Spread mixture evenly into greased 11×7-inch baking dish. Bake 20 minutes. Cool on wire rack 20 minutes before cutting into squares. Serve warm or at room temperature. Refrigerate leftovers. *Makes 12 servings*

Chicken Tortilla Soup

4 (6-inch) flour tortillas, cut into thin strips
3 cups water
3 teaspoons HERB-OX® chicken flavored bouillon
1 (1¼-ounce) package taco seasoning mix
1 (16-ounce) jar CHI-CHI'S® Salsa
2 (10-ounce) cans HORMEL® chunk breast of chicken, drained and flaked
1 (15-ounce) can black beans, drained and rinsed
1 (11-ounce) can corn with red and green bell peppers
Sour cream, if desired

Place tortilla strips onto baking pan. Lightly spray strips with nonstick cooking spray. Bake at 400°F until crisp, about 10 minutes. Meanwhile, in large saucepan, combine water, bouillon, taco seasoning mix and salsa. Bring mixture to a boil. Reduce heat and simmer for 5 minutes. Add chunk chicken, black beans and corn. Heat until warmed through, about 10 minutes. Ladle into warm bowls and top with tortilla crisps and sour cream, if desired.   *Makes 6 servings*

CHUNKY ANCHO CHILI WITH BEANS

- 5 dried ancho chiles
- 2 cups water
- 2 tablespoons vegetable oil or lard
- 1 large onion, chopped
- 2 cloves garlic, minced
- 1 pound boneless beef top sirloin steak, cut into 1-inch cubes
- 1 pound boneless pork, cut into 1-inch cubes
- 1 to 2 fresh or canned jalapeño peppers,* stemmed, seeded and minced
- 1 teaspoon salt
- 1 teaspoon dried oregano
- 1 teaspoon ground cumin
- ½ cup dry red wine
- 3 cups cooked pinto beans *or* 2 cans (15 ounces each) pinto or kidney beans, drained

*Jalapeño peppers can sting and irritate the skin; wear rubber gloves when handling peppers and do not touch eyes. Wash hands after handling.

1. Rinse ancho chiles; remove stems, seeds and veins. Place in 2-quart pan with water. Bring to a boil; turn off heat and let stand, covered, 30 minutes or until chiles are soft. Pour chiles with liquid into blender or food processor container fitted with metal blade. Process until smooth; reserve.

2. Heat oil in 5-quart Dutch oven over medium heat. Add onion and garlic; cook until onion is tender. Add beef and pork; cook, stirring frequently, until meat is lightly browned. Add jalapeño peppers, salt, oregano, cumin, wine and ancho chile purée. Bring to a boil. Cover; reduce heat and simmer 1½ to 2 hours or until meat is very tender. Stir in beans. Simmer, uncovered, 30 minutes or until chili has thickened slightly. *Makes 8 servings*

VARIATION: To make chili with chili powder, use ⅓ cup chili powder and 1½ cups water in place of ancho chile purée. Reduce salt and cumin to ½ teaspoon each.

CHUNKY ANCHO CHILI WITH BEANS

BLACK BEAN SOUP

2 tablespoons vegetable oil

1 large onion, chopped

3 large cloves garlic, minced

4 cans (15 to 19 ounces each) black beans, undrained

2 cans (14½ ounces each) reduced-sodium chicken broth

⅓ cup *Frank's® RedHot®* Original Cayenne Pepper Sauce

¼ cup minced fresh cilantro

2 teaspoons ground cumin

1. Heat oil in 4- to 5-quart saucepan. Add onion and garlic; cook until tender. Stir in beans with liquid, broth, *Frank's RedHot* Sauce, cilantro and cumin.

2. Bring to a boil. Reduce heat; simmer, partially covered, 30 minutes, stirring often.

3. Remove 1 cup soup. Place in blender; cover securely and process until smooth. Return to saucepan; stir. Serve soup in individual soup bowls. Top with dollop of sour cream, if desired. *Makes 10 servings*

NOTE: This soup freezes well. Freeze leftovers in individual portions. Thaw and reheat in microwave oven.

PREP TIME: 10 minutes
COOK TIME: 35 minutes

TEXAS CHILI & BISCUITS

1 pound ground beef
1 package (about 1¾ ounces) chili seasoning mix
1 can (16 ounces) whole kernel corn, drained
1 can (14½ ounces) whole tomatoes, undrained
   and cut up
½ cup water
¾ cup biscuit baking mix
⅔ cup cornmeal
⅔ cup milk
1⅓ cups *French's®* French Fried Onions, divided
½ cup (2 ounces) shredded Monterey Jack cheese

Preheat oven to 400°F. In medium skillet, brown beef;
drain. Stir in chili seasoning, corn, tomatoes and water;
bring to a boil. Reduce heat; simmer, uncovered, 10 minutes.
Meanwhile, in medium bowl, combine baking mix, cornmeal,
milk and ⅔ *cup* French Fried Onions; beat vigorously
30 seconds. Pour beef mixture into 2-quart casserole. Spoon
biscuit dough in mounds around edge of casserole. Bake,
uncovered, at 400°F for 15 minutes or until biscuits are light
brown. Top biscuits with cheese and remaining ⅔ *cup* onions;
bake, uncovered, 1 to 3 minutes or until onions are golden
brown. *Makes 4 to 6 servings*

Chilis, Soups & Breads 47

CHILI MOLE

1 pound ground beef
1 Spanish onion, diced
1 green bell pepper, diced
1 banana pepper, finely chopped
2 jalapeño peppers,* finely chopped
2 cloves garlic, finely chopped
2 cans (15 ounces each) kidney beans, rinsed and
   drained
2 cans (14½ ounces each) diced tomatoes, undrained
1 can (4 ounces) tomato paste
1 packet (2 ounces) Cincinnati-style chili seasoning
2 tablespoons chili powder
3 tablespoons unsweetened cocoa powder
1 tablespoon brown sugar
1 tablespoon lime juice

*Jalapeño peppers can sting and irritate the skin; wear rubber gloves when handling peppers and do not touch eyes. Wash hands after handling.

1. Brown ground beef in large Dutch oven over medium-high heat, stirring to separate meat. Drain and discard fat.

2. Add onion and bell pepper. Cook and stir until onion is translucent.

3. Add banana pepper, jalapeños and garlic; cook and stir 3 minutes.

4. Add beans and tomatoes with juice. Stir in tomato paste, chili seasoning, chili powder, cocoa, brown sugar and lime juice. Cover; simmer 1 hour. *Makes 6 servings*

BLUE CORN MUFFINS

Honey Butter (recipe follows)
1 cup all-purpose flour
¾ cup blue cornmeal
2 tablespoons sugar
1½ teaspoons baking powder
½ teaspoon baking soda
¼ teaspoon salt
1 cup buttermilk or sour cream
2 eggs
¼ cup (½ stick) butter, melted

1. Prepare Honey Butter. Preheat oven to 400°F. Grease or paper line 12 (2½-inch) muffin cups.

2. Combine flour, cornmeal, sugar, baking powder, baking soda and salt. Whisk buttermilk, eggs and butter in small bowl until blended. Pour buttermilk mixture into dry ingredients; stir just until moistened. Fill each prepared muffin cup ⅔ full with batter.

3. Bake 15 to 20 minutes or until toothpick inserted into centers comes out clean. Remove muffins from pan to wire rack; cool 5 minutes. Serve warm muffins with Honey Butter.

Makes 12 muffins

BLUE CORN STICKS: Preheat corn stick pans in 400°F oven 5 minutes. Melt ½ teaspoon butter in each section. Fill each section ¾ full with batter. Bake 12 to 15 minutes or until toothpick inserted into centers comes out clean.

HONEY BUTTER

½ cup (1 stick) butter, softened
⅓ cup honey
1 teaspoon grated orange peel

Beat butter until fluffy. Add honey; beat until well blended. Stir in orange peel.

Makes about ¾ cup

WHITE CHICKEN CHILI

6 cups water

6 cubes HERB-OX® chicken flavored bouillon

2 teaspoons ground cumin

1 teaspoon lemon pepper

1 pound boneless, skinless chicken breasts, diced

1 medium yellow onion, chopped

1 (15-ounce) can hominy, drained

1 (15-ounce) can Great Northern beans, rinsed
   and drained

1 (7-ounce) can white corn, drained

1 (4.25-ounce) can CHI-CHI'S® diced green chilies

Crushed tortilla chips

Shredded Monterey Jack cheese

Guacamole

In large saucepan, combine water, bouillon, cumin, lemon
pepper and chopped chicken. Bring mixture to a boil; reduce
heat, cover and simmer 8 to 10 minutes or until chicken is
cooked through. Add onion, hominy, beans, corn, and green
chilies. Cook until thoroughly heated, 10 to 15 minutes. If
desired, top with crushed tortilla chips, shredded cheese
and guacamole.   *Makes 10 to 12 servings*

PREP TIME: 15 minutes
TOTAL TIME: 50 minutes

tip Not enough time to cook? Portion cooled, leftover
chili into individual food storage containers. Cover
tightly and freeze. For a last minute meal, pop a container in the
microwave to thaw and reheat.

Chilis, Soups & Breads ◆ *51*

CHIPOTLE CHILI CON CARNE

1 tablespoon chili powder

1 tablespoon ground cumin

¾ pound beef for stew, cut into 1-inch pieces

Nonstick cooking spray

1 can (about 14 ounces) beef broth

1 tablespoon minced canned chipotle chiles in adobo sauce, or to taste

1 can (14½ ounces) diced tomatoes, undrained

1 large green bell pepper *or* 2 poblano peppers, cut into ½-inch pieces

2 cans (15 ounces each) pinto or red beans, rinsed and drained

Chopped fresh cilantro (optional)

1. Combine chili powder and cumin in medium bowl. Add beef; toss to coat. Coat large saucepan or Dutch oven with cooking spray; heat over medium heat. Add beef; cook and stir 5 minutes. Add beef broth and chipotles with sauce; bring to a boil. Reduce heat; cover and simmer 1 hour 15 minutes or until beef is very tender.

2. With slotted spoon, transfer beef to carving board, leaving juices in saucepan. Using two forks, shred beef. Return beef to saucepan; add tomatoes with juice and bell pepper. Bring to a boil; stir in beans. Simmer, uncovered, 20 minutes or until bell pepper is tender. Garnish with cilantro, if desired.

Makes 6 servings

PREP TIME: 15 minutes
COOK TIME: 1 hour 40 minutes

CHIPOTLE CHILI CON CARNE

TEX-MEX CHEDDAR CHEESE SOUP

2 cans (10¾ ounces each) condensed Cheddar cheese or cream of chicken soup
2 cups milk
1 cup half and half
2 cups shredded Cheddar cheese
1 can (4 ounces) green chilies, finely chopped
1 teaspoon ground cumin
2 cups French's® French Fried Onions

1. Combine soup, milk and cream in large saucepan. Heat over medium-high heat until hot. Stir in cheese, chilies and cumin. Cook until cheese melts, stirring constantly.

2. Place French Fried Onions on microwave-safe dish. Microwave on HIGH 1 minute or until golden.

3. Spoon soup into bowls. Garnish with sour cream and fresh cilantro if desired. Top with onions. *Makes 6 servings*

PREP TIME: 5 minutes
COOK TIME: 10 minutes

POZOLE

1½ pounds boneless fresh pork butt roast

1 large onion, coarsely chopped

2 cloves garlic, minced

1 bay leaf

1 dried red New Mexico or California chile, seeds removed, *or* 1 teaspoon red chili powder

1 teaspoon dried oregano leaves

½ teaspoon cumin seeds

½ teaspoon coriander seeds

½ teaspoon black peppercorns

10 cups water

3 chicken legs with thighs attached

1 can (29 ounces) yellow or white hominy, drained

CONDIMENTS

3 limes, cut into wedges

1 package (3 ounces) cream cheese, cut into cubes

½ head iceberg lettuce, shredded

1 bunch radishes, thinly sliced

6 green onions with tops, thinly sliced

1 avocado, peeled, pitted and finely chopped

1. Combine pork, onion, garlic, bay leaf, chile, oregano, cumin seeds, coriander seeds, peppercorns and water in 5-quart Dutch oven. Bring to a boil. Cover; reduce heat and simmer 45 minutes. Add chicken. Simmer 1 hour or until meat is tender. Remove meat with slotted spoon to pan; let cool. Pour broth through sieve set over large bowl; discard solids. Return broth to Dutch oven. Skim fat. (If making ahead, cool, cover and refrigerate overnight; remove fat.) When meat is cool enough to handle, discard skin and bones; shred meat. Cover and refrigerate until needed.

2. Reheat broth to simmering. Add hominy. Cover and simmer 30 minutes. Return meat to broth; heat to simmering. Spoon pozole into individual bowls. Serve with condiments.

Makes 6 servings

Chilis, Soups & Breads ◈ 55

THREE-BEAN MOLE CHILI

1 can (15½ ounces) chili beans in spicy sauce, undrained
1 can (15 ounces) pinto beans, rinsed and drained
1 can (15 ounces) black beans, rinsed and drained
1 can (14½ ounces) Mexican or chili-style diced
    tomatoes, undrained
1 large green bell pepper, diced
1 small onion, diced
½ cup beef, chicken or vegetable broth
¼ cup prepared mole paste*
2 teaspoons ground cumin
2 teaspoons chili powder
2 teaspoons ground coriander (optional)
2 teaspoons minced garlic
    Toppings: crushed tortilla chips, chopped cilantro or
    shredded cheese

*Mole paste is available in the Mexican section of large supermarkets or in specialty markets.

SLOW COOKER DIRECTIONS

1. Combine beans, tomatoes with juice, bell pepper, onion, broth, mole paste, cumin, chili powder, coriander and garlic in slow cooker; mix well.

2. Cover; cook on LOW 5 to 6 hours or until vegetables are tender.

3. Serve with desired toppings.   *Makes 4 to 6 servings*

PREP TIME: 10 minutes
COOK TIME: 5 to 6 hours (LOW)

THREE-BEAN MOLE CHILI

Stuffed Tortillas

SPEEDY BEEF & BEAN BURRITOS

8 (7-inch) flour tortillas
1 pound ground beef
1 cup chopped onion
1 teaspoon minced garlic
1 can (15 ounces) black beans, rinsed and drained
1 cup chunky salsa
2 teaspoons ground cumin
¼ cup chopped fresh cilantro
2 cups (8 ounces) shredded Monterey Jack cheese

1. Preheat oven to 350°F. Wrap tortillas in foil; place on center rack in oven. Heat tortillas 15 minutes.

2. Meanwhile, combine beef, onion and garlic in large skillet. Cook and stir over medium-high heat, stirring to separate meat; drain fat.

3. Stir beans, salsa and cumin into beef mixture. Cover and simmer over medium heat 10 minutes, stirring once.

4. Stir cilantro into filling. Spoon filling down centers of warm tortillas; top with cheese. Roll up and serve immediately.

Makes 4 servings

PREP AND COOK TIME: 20 minutes

SPEEDY BEEF & BEAN BURRITOS

58

FIESTA BEEF ENCHILADAS

½ pound (8 ounces) ground beef
½ cup sliced green onions
2 teaspoons minced garlic
1 cup cooked white or brown rice
1½ cups chopped tomato, divided
¾ cup frozen corn, thawed
1 cup (4 ounces) shredded Mexican cheese blend
or Cheddar cheese, divided
½ cup salsa or picante sauce
12 (6- to 7-inch) corn tortillas
1 can (10 ounces) mild or hot enchilada sauce
1 cup shredded romaine lettuce

1. Preheat oven to 375°F. Spray 13×9-inch baking dish with nonstick cooking spray; set aside.

2. Brown ground beef in large nonstick skillet over medium-high heat, stirring to separate meat; drain fat. Add green onions and garlic; cook and stir 2 minutes.

3. Add rice, 1 cup tomato, corn, ½ cup cheese and salsa to meat mixture; mix well. Spoon mixture down center of tortillas. Roll up; place seam side down in prepared dish. Spoon enchilada sauce evenly over enchiladas.

4. Cover with foil; bake 20 minutes or until hot. Sprinkle with remaining ½ cup cheese; bake 5 minutes or until cheese melts. Top with lettuce and remaining ½ cup tomato.

Makes 6 servings

PREP TIME: 15 minutes
COOK TIME: 35 minutes

FIESTA BEEF ENCHILADAS

Stuffed Tortillas

1 can (8 ounces) tomato sauce

⅓ cup prepared salsa or picante sauce

¼ cup chopped fresh cilantro or thinly sliced green
onions

4 large eggs

Butter or margarine

4 (6-inch) corn tortillas, crisply fried or 4 prepared
tostada shells

1 cup (4 ounces) SARGENTO® Taco Blend Shredded
Cheese

Combine tomato sauce, salsa and cilantro; heat in microwave
oven or in saucepan over medium-high heat until hot. Fry
eggs in butter, sunny side up. Place one egg on each tortilla;
top with sauce. Sprinkle with cheese. **_Makes 4 servings_**

VARIATION: Spread tortillas with heated refried beans before
topping with eggs, if desired.

tip Tostadas start with a crisp, flat fried tortilla which
is then covered with various toppings. To keep the
tortilla flavor but reduce the fat, use soft corn tortillas as the
base for eggs and sauce. Instead of frying, just heat tortillas in
a nonstick skillet until browned. Or, place tortillas on a baking
sheet. Spray both sides of tortillas with nonstick cooking spray.
Bake in a 450°F oven for 5 minutes or until lightly browned
and crisp.

CHEESY CHICKEN ENCHILADAS

¼ cup (½ stick) butter

1 cup chopped onion

2 cloves garlic, minced

¼ cup all-purpose flour

1 cup chicken broth

4 ounces cream cheese, softened

2 cups (8 ounces) shredded Mexican cheese blend, divided

1 cup shredded cooked chicken

1 can (7 ounces) chopped green chilies, drained

½ cup diced pimientos

6 (8-inch) flour tortillas, warmed

¼ cup chopped fresh cilantro

¾ cup prepared salsa

1. Preheat oven to 350°F. Spray 13×9-inch baking dish with nonstick cooking spray.

2. Melt butter in medium saucepan over medium heat. Add onion and garlic; cook and stir until onion is tender. Add flour; cook and stir 1 minute. Gradually whisk in chicken broth; cook and stir 2 to 3 minutes or until slightly thickened. Add cream cheese; stir until melted. Stir in ½ cup shredded cheese, chicken, chilies and pimientos.

3. Spoon about ⅓ cup mixture onto each tortilla. Roll up and place seam side down in prepared baking dish. Pour remaining mixture over enchiladas; sprinkle with remaining 1½ cups shredded cheese.

4. Bake 20 minutes or until bubbly and lightly browned. Sprinkle with cilantro and serve with salsa.

Makes 6 servings

DOUBLE DUTY TACOS

MEXICALI CHILI RUB
- ¼ cup chili powder
- 3 tablespoons garlic salt
- 2 tablespoons ground cumin
- 2 tablespoons dried oregano leaves
- ½ teaspoon ground red pepper

TACOS
- 2 pounds ground beef
- 1 large onion, chopped
- 3 tablespoons Mexicali Chili Rub
- ¾ cup water
- 2 tablespoons tomato paste
- 16 packaged crispy taco shells
- 2 cups (8 ounces) shredded Monterey Jack or taco-flavored cheese
- 2 cups shredded lettuce
- 1 cup chopped tomatoes
- 1 cup diced ripe avocado
- ½ cup sour cream
- Prepared salsa

1. For rub, combine chili powder, garlic salt, cumin, oregano and ground red pepper in small bowl; mix well. Transfer to container with tight-fitting lid. Store in cool dry place up to 2 months.

2. Brown beef and onion in large deep skillet over medium-high heat, stirring to separate meat. Drain and discard fat. Sprinkle chili rub over beef mixture; cook 1 minute. Reduce heat to medium. Add water and tomato paste. Cover; simmer 5 minutes.

3. Spoon beef mixture into taco shells; top with cheese. Arrange lettuce, tomatoes, avocado, sour cream and salsa in bowls. Serve tacos with toppings.   *Makes 8 servings*

DOUBLE DUTY TACOS

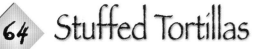

TEX-MEX TOSTADAS

4 (8-inch) flour tortillas
  Nonstick cooking spray
1 green bell pepper, diced
¾ pound boneless skinless chicken breasts,
  cut into strips
1½ teaspoons minced garlic
1 teaspoon chili powder
1 teaspoon ground cumin
½ cup chunky salsa, divided
⅓ cup sliced green onions
1 cup canned refried beans
1 medium tomato, diced
¼ cup sour cream (optional)

1. Preheat oven to 450°F. Place tortillas on baking sheet; coat both sides with cooking spray. Bake 5 minutes or until lightly browned and crisp. Set aside.

2. Coat large nonstick skillet with cooking spray. Add bell pepper; cook and stir 4 minutes. Add chicken, garlic, chili powder and cumin; cook and stir 4 minutes or until chicken is no longer pink in center. Add ¼ cup salsa and green onions; cook and stir 1 minute. Remove skillet from heat; set aside.

3. Combine refried beans and remaining ¼ cup salsa in microwavable bowl. Cook, uncovered, at HIGH 1½ minutes or until beans are heated through.

4. Spread bean mixture evenly over tortillas. Spoon chicken mixture and tomato over bean mixture. Garnish with sour cream, if desired. *Makes 4 servings*

TEX-MEX TOSTADA

CHICKEN ENCHILADA ROLL-UPS

1½ pounds boneless skinless chicken breasts
½ cup plus 2 tablespoons all-purpose flour, divided
½ teaspoon salt
2 tablespoons butter
1 cup chicken broth
1 small onion, diced
¼ to ½ cup canned jalapeño peppers, sliced
½ teaspoon dried oregano leaves
2 tablespoons heavy cream or milk
6 flour tortillas (7 to 8 inches)
6 thin slices American cheese or American cheese
   with jalapeño peppers

SLOW COOKER DIRECTIONS

1. Cut each chicken breast lengthwise into 2 or 3 strips. Combine ½ cup flour and salt in resealable plastic food storage bag. Add chicken strips and shake to coat with flour mixture. Melt butter in large skillet over medium heat. Brown chicken strips in batches 2 to 3 minutes per side. Place chicken in slow cooker.

2. Add chicken broth to skillet and scrape up any browned bits. Pour broth mixture into slow cooker. Add onion, jalapeño peppers and oregano. Cover; cook on LOW 7 to 8 hours or on HIGH 3 to 4 hours.

3. Blend remaining 2 tablespoons flour and cream in small bowl until smooth. Stir into chicken mixture. Cook, uncovered, on HIGH 15 minutes or until thickened. Spoon chicken mixture onto center of flour tortillas. Top with 1 cheese slice. Fold up tortillas and serve.

Makes 6 servings

SERVING SUGGESTION: This rich creamy chicken mixture can also be served over hot cooked rice.

PREP TIME: 20 minutes
COOK TIME: 7 to 8 hours (LOW) • 3 to 4 hours (HIGH)

Stuffed Tortillas

LAMB ENCHILADAS WITH GREEN SAUCE

1 can (13 ounces) tomatillos, rinsed and drained
1 can (4 ounces) chopped green chilies, drained
¼ cup chopped onion
2 sprigs cilantro or parsley
2 cloves garlic, minced, divided
½ cup chicken broth
1 teaspoon sugar
   Dash pepper
½ pound lean American Ground Lamb
½ cup chopped green pepper
¼ cup chopped celery
8 (6-inch) flour tortillas
½ cup shredded mozzarella or Monterey Jack cheese
   (2 ounces)

For Green Sauce, in blender container or food processor bowl combine tomatillos, chilies, onion, cilantro and 1 clove garlic. Blend or process till smooth. Pour into small saucepan. Add broth, sugar and pepper. Bring to a boil; reduce heat. Simmer, covered, 10 minutes.

In skillet cook lamb, 1 clove garlic, green pepper and celery until no pink remains and vegetables are crisp-tender. Drain off any fat. To soften tortillas, stack with white paper toweling between each tortilla. Microwave on HIGH 1 to 2 minutes or until tortillas are pliable. (Or, if desired, wrap tortillas in foil. Heat in 350°F oven about 10 minutes or until pliable). Spoon meat mixture onto each tortilla, then roll up. Place filled tortillas, seam-side down, in 11×7-inch baking dish. Top with Green Sauce. Cover with foil. Bake in 350°F oven for 20 minutes. Uncover; sprinkle with cheese. Return to oven for 5 minutes. Serve garnished with sour cream and green onion.

Makes 4 servings

RED SAUCE OPTION: Substitute salsa or taco sauce for the Green Sauce above. Prepare and serve as above.

*Favorite recipe from **American Lamb Council***

Stuffed Tortillas ◇ 69

Enticing Enchiladas

1 tablespoon vegetable oil
1 green or red bell pepper, chopped
½ cup chopped onion
4 cloves garlic, minced
1 package JENNIE-O TURKEY STORE® Lean
   Ground Turkey
1 tablespoon Mexican seasoning or chili powder
2 cans (10 ounces) mild enchilada sauce, divided
2 cups (8 ounces) shredded Mexican cheese blend
   or Monterey Jack cheese, divided
12 (7-inch) soft flour tortillas or flavored flour tortillas
1 cup shredded lettuce
½ cup diced tomato
   Ripe avocado slices (optional)

Heat oven to 375°F. Heat oil in large skillet over medium heat.
Add bell pepper, onion and garlic; cook 5 minutes, stirring
occasionally. Crumble turkey into skillet; sprinkle with
seasoning. Cook about 8 minutes or until no longer pink,
stirring occasionally. Stir in ½ cup enchilada sauce. Remove
from heat; stir in 1 cup cheese. Spread ½ cup enchilada sauce
over bottom of 13×9-inch baking dish. Spoon about ⅓ cup
turkey mixture down center of each tortilla. Fold bottom of
tortilla up over filling, fold in sides and roll up. Place seam side
down in prepared dish. Spoon remaining enchilada sauce
evenly over enchiladas. Cover with foil; bake 20 minutes.
Sprinkle with remaining 1 cup cheese. Return to oven; bake,
uncovered, 10 minutes or until cheese is melted and sauce is
bubbly. Garnish with lettuce and tomato. Top with avocado,
if desired.   *Makes 6 servings*

Prep Time: 30 minutes
Cook Time: 45 minutes

Enticing Enchiladas

Stuffed Tortillas

ORIGINAL ORTEGA® TACO RECIPE

    1 pound ground beef
    1 package (1¼ ounces) ORTEGA® Taco Seasoning Mix
    ¾ cup water
    1 package (12) ORTEGA Taco Shells, warmed

SUGGESTED TOPPINGS
    Shredded lettuce, chopped tomatoes, shredded
        cheddar cheese, ORTEGA Thick & Smooth Taco
        Sauce

BROWN beef; drain. Stir in seasoning mix and water; bring to a boil. Reduce heat to low; cook, stirring occasionally, for 5 to 6 minutes or until mixture is thickened.

FILL taco shells with beef mixture. Top with desired toppings.

Makes 6 servings

Pork Burritos

1 boneless fresh pork butt roast (about 2½ pounds)
1 cup chopped white onion
1 carrot, sliced
1 clove garlic, minced
½ teaspoon salt
½ teaspoon ground cumin
½ teaspoon coriander seeds, lightly crushed
   Water
   Fresh Tomato Salsa (page 12)
12 flour tortillas (8-inch diameter)
 2 cups canned refried beans
 2 medium avocados, peeled, pitted, diced
 1 cup (4 ounces) shredded Monterey Jack cheese

1. Place pork, onion, carrot, garlic, salt, cumin and coriander seeds in 5-quart Dutch oven. Add just enough water to cover pork. Bring to a boil over high heat. Reduce heat to low. Cover; simmer 2 to 2½ hours until pork is tender.

2. Prepare Fresh Tomato Salsa.

3. Preheat oven to 350°F. Remove pork from Dutch oven; set aside. Strain cooking liquid through cheesecloth-lined sieve; reserve ½ cup liquid.

4. Place pork on rack in roasting pan. Roast 40 to 45 minutes until well browned, turning once. Let stand until cool enough to handle.

5. Trim and discard outer fat from pork. Using 2 forks, pull pork into coarse shreds. Combine pork and reserved cooking liquid in medium skillet. Heat over medium heat 5 minutes or until meat is hot and moistly coated with liquid; stir often.

6. Soften and warm tortillas.

7. Place about 2½ tablespoons beans on bottom half of 1 tortilla; spread out slightly. Layer with pork, salsa, diced avocado and cheese.

8. Fold right edge of tortilla up over filling; fold bottom edge over filling, then loosely roll up, leaving one end of burrito open. Repeat until all burritos are filled.　*Makes 6 servings*

TACOS CON PUERCO

   1 pound ground pork
   1 can (8 ounces) whole tomatoes, undrained, cut up
   ¼ cup chopped onion
   1 tablespoon chili powder
   ¼ teaspoon garlic powder
      Salt and pepper
   8 taco shells
   2 fresh tomatoes, cut into wedges
   2 cups shredded iceberg lettuce

In heavy skillet, brown ground pork; stir in undrained canned tomatoes, onion, chili powder and garlic powder. Bring to a boil; reduce heat and simmer, uncovered, until most liquid evaporates, about 15 minutes, stirring occasionally. Season to taste with salt and pepper. Heat taco shells according to package directions. Portion filling into shells; top with fresh tomatoes and lettuce.　*Makes 4 servings*

PREP TIME: 10 minutes
COOK TIME: 15 minutes

*Favorite recipe from **National Pork Board***

Green Chile Chicken Enchiladas

2 cups shredded cooked chicken

**1½ cups (6 ounces) shredded Mexican cheese blend
     or Cheddar cheese, divided**

½ cup HIDDEN VALLEY® The Original Ranch® Dressing

¼ cup sour cream

**2 tablespoons canned diced green chiles, rinsed
     and drained**

4 (9- to 10-inch) flour tortillas, warmed

Mix together chicken, ¾ cup cheese, dressing, sour cream
and green chiles in medium bowl. Divide evenly down center
of each tortilla. Roll up tortillas and place, seam side down, in
9-inch baking dish. Top with remaining ¾ cup cheese. Bake at
350°F. for 20 minutes or until cheese is melted and lightly
browned.   *Makes 4 servings*

NOTE: Purchase rotisserie chicken at your favorite store to add
great taste and save preparation time.

GREEN CHILE CHICKEN ENCHILADA

BEEF AND BEAN CHIMICHANGAS

1 pound ground beef
2 tablespoons CRISCO® Oil
1 medium onion, chopped
2 cloves garlic, minced
1 small red bell pepper, diced
1 can (16 ounces) whole tomatoes, drained
　　and chopped
⅓ cup salsa
1½ teaspoons chili powder
¾ teaspoon ground coriander
½ teaspoon ground thyme
½ teaspoon salt
⅛ teaspoon cayenne
⅛ teaspoon ground cumin
1 cup refried beans
1 cup cooked black beans
6 (8-inch) flour tortillas
　　CRISCO® Oil for frying
¾ cup shredded Monterey Jack cheese
　　Shredded iceberg lettuce (optional)
　　Additional salsa (optional)
　　Purchased guacamole (optional)
　　Sour cream (optional)

Place ground beef in medium skillet. Brown over medium-high heat. Drain. Remove beef from skillet; set aside. Place 2 tablespoons CRISCO® Oil in medium skillet. Add onion, garlic and red bell pepper. Cook and stir over moderate heat until onion is tender. Stir in ground beef, tomatoes, salsa, chili powder, coriander, thyme, salt, cayenne and cumin. Cook over medium-low heat, stirring occasionally, 10 to 15 minutes, or until mixture is thickened. Remove from heat. Stir in refried beans and black beans.

continued on page 80

BEEF AND BEAN CHIMICHANGA

Stuffed Tortillas

Beef and Bean Chimichangas, continued

Place ½ cup beef mixture in center of each tortilla. Fold opposite sides of tortilla toward center over beef mixture. Fold ends toward center; secure with wooden pick. Chill 15 minutes.

Heat 2 inches CRISCO® Oil in deep-fryer or large saucepan to 375°F.

Fry 1 or 2 chimichangas at a time 1½ to 2 minutes or until golden brown. Drain on paper towels. Sprinkle top of each chimichanga with 2 tablespoons Monterey Jack cheese. Serve immediately on a bed of shredded iceberg lettuce with salsa, guacamole and sour cream, if desired. *Makes 6 servings*

PREP TIME: 25 minutes
TOTAL TIME: 60 minutes

SHREDDED PORK TACOS

> 3 cups shredded or finely chopped cooked roast pork
> 1 cup chopped onion
> 1 clove garlic, minced
> 1 to 3 tablespoons diced jalapeño pepper
> 12 small flour tortillas, warmed
> 3 cups shredded lettuce
> 2 cups diced tomatoes
> ¾ cup (3 ounces) shredded Cheddar cheese
> Salsa (optional)

In medium nonstick skillet, cook and stir onion and garlic over medium heat 5 minutes until soft and translucent. Add cooked pork; toss lightly. Heat thoroughly; stir in jalapeño pepper. On each tortilla, spoon ¼ cup shredded pork, a portion of lettuce, tomatoes and 1 tablespoon cheese; top with salsa, if desired.
Makes 6 servings

PREP TIME: 15 minutes

*Favorite recipe from **National Pork Board***

Stuffed Tortillas

Fiesta Beef Enchiladas

6 ounces ground beef

¼ cup sliced green onions

1 teaspoon minced garlic

1 cup (4 ounces) shredded Mexican cheese blend
  or Cheddar cheese, divided

¾ cup chopped tomato, divided

½ cup frozen corn, thawed

⅓ cup cooked white or brown rice

¼ cup salsa or picante sauce

6 (6- to 7-inch) corn tortillas

2 sheets (20×12 inches) heavy-duty foil, generously
  sprayed with nonstick cooking spray

½ cup mild or hot red or green enchilada sauce

½ cup sliced romaine lettuce leaves

1. Preheat oven to 375°F.

2. Brown ground beef in medium nonstick skillet over medium-high heat, stirring to separate. Drain and discard fat. Add green onions and garlic; cook and stir 2 minutes.

3. Combine meat mixture, ¾ cup cheese, ½ cup tomato, corn, rice and salsa; mix well. Spoon mixture down center of tortillas. Roll up; place, seam side down, on foil sheet, three to a sheet. Spoon enchilada sauce evenly over enchiladas.

4. Double fold sides and ends of foil to seal packets, leaving head space for heat circulation. Place packets on baking sheet.

5. Bake 15 minutes or until hot. Remove from oven; open packets. Sprinkle with remaining ¼ cup cheese; seal packet. Bake 10 minutes more. Transfer contents to serving plates; serve with lettuce and remaining ¼ cup tomato.

Makes 2 servings

Prep Time: 15 minutes
Cook Time: 25 minutes

Stuffed Tortillas 81

Turkey Tostadas

1 package BUTTERBALL® Fresh Boneless Turkey
    Breast Strips
1 tablespoon vegetable oil
1 tablespoon chili powder
½ teaspoon salt
8 (6-inch) tostadas or corn tortillas
1 cup fat free vegetarian refried beans
2 cups shredded iceberg lettuce
1 cup (4 ounces) shredded low fat Cheddar cheese
1 avocado, coarsely chopped
1 cup chopped tomato
½ cup chopped green onions

Heat oil in large nonstick skillet over medium heat until hot.
Add turkey strips; sprinkle with chili powder and salt. Cook
and stir frequently about 5 minutes or until no longer pink.
Spread each tostada with 2 tablespoons refried beans. Divide
shredded lettuce evenly among tostadas. Place cooked turkey
strips on top of lettuce; sprinkle with cheese. Add avocado,
tomato and onions to each tostada. Serve with low fat sour
cream and salsa, if desired. *Makes 8 tostadas*

Tip: To assure safe, tender, juicy fresh cuts, cook turkey until
no longer pink in center, being careful not to overcook.

Prep Time: 20 minutes

Turkey Tostada

Stuffed Tortillas

CHEESE ENCHILADAS

   Red Chili Sauce (page 85)
   Vegetable oil for frying
 12 (6- or 7-inch) corn tortillas
   3 cups (12 ounces) shredded Monterey Jack cheese
   1 medium onion, chopped
   3 green onions with tops, thinly sliced

1. Prepare Red Chili Sauce.

2. Preheat oven to 350°F. Heat ½ inch oil in 7- to 8-inch skillet over medium-high heat. Place 1 tortilla in hot oil; cook 2 seconds on each side or just until limp. Drain briefly on paper towels.

3. Dip softened tortilla into chili sauce. Transfer sauced tortilla to plate. Place about 3 tablespoons cheese and 2 teaspoons chopped onion across center of tortilla; roll to enclose. Place enchiladas, seam side down, in 15×10-inch baking pan. Repeat until all tortillas are filled. Spoon remaining chili sauce over enchiladas, making sure ends are moistened. Sprinkle with remaining cheese.

4. Bake, covered, 20 to 30 minutes or until hot in center. Sprinkle with green onions just before serving.

Makes 6 servings

QUICK ENCHILADAS: Use 1 large can (19 ounces) and 1 small can (10 ounces) enchilada sauce in place of Red Chili Sauce. Omit step of dipping tortillas into hot oil; instead dip each tortilla directly into enough warm enchilada sauce to soften tortilla so it rolls easily. Fill and bake as directed above.

Stuffed Tortillas

RED CHILI SAUCE

3 tablespoons olive oil or vegetable oil
1 clove garlic, minced
2 tablespoons all-purpose flour
⅓ cup mild chili powder
2 cups water
1 teaspoon dried oregano
½ teaspoon salt

1. Heat oil in 3-quart pan over low heat. Add garlic; cook 2 minutes or just until golden. Add flour and cook, stirring constantly, until mixture is bubbling and a light golden color.

2. Blend in chili powder. Stir in water; add oregano and salt. Increase heat to medium; cook, stirring constantly, until sauce is thick and boiling. Reduce heat to low so sauce stays warm but does not boil. *Makes 2 cups*

RED CHILI SAUCE FROM DRIED RED CHILES: Wash 16 to 20 dried red New Mexico or California chiles; remove stems and seeds. Place in 3-quart pan with 3 cups water. Cover and simmer 20 minutes or until chiles are very soft. Pour chiles and liquid into blender or food processor container fitted with metal blade; process until puréed. Push purée through wire strainer; discard pulp. Heat 1 tablespoon vegetable oil in large skillet over medium heat. Add ⅓ cup finely chopped onion and 1 clove garlic, minced; cook until onion is tender. Add chile purée, 1 teaspoon dried oregano and ¾ teaspoon salt. Simmer 10 minutes. Makes about 2½ cups

tip Fix enchiladas when you're preparing dinner for a crowd. Just like lasagna, enchilada dishes hold well on buffets, can be prepared in large quantities ahead of time and baked right before serving. With an enchilada casserole on the menu, you'll have enough time to get everything done for the party!

Stuffed Tortillas ◆ **85**

Spicy Beef Tacos

1 pound boneless beef chuck, cut into 1-inch cubes
Vegetable oil
1 to 2 teaspoons chili powder
1 clove garlic, minced
½ teaspoon salt
½ teaspoon ground cumin
1 can (14½ ounces) diced tomatoes, undrained
12 (6-inch) corn tortillas*
1 cup (4 ounces) shredded mild Cheddar cheese
2 to 3 cups shredded iceberg lettuce
1 large fresh tomato, seeded, chopped
Cilantro for garnish

*Or, substitute packaged taco shells for the corn tortillas. Omit steps 4 and 5. Warm taco shells according to package directions.

1. Brown beef in 2 tablespoons hot oil in large skillet over medium-high heat 10 to 12 minutes, turning frequently. Reduce heat to low. Stir in chili powder, garlic, salt and cumin. Cook and stir 30 seconds.

2. Add canned tomatoes with juice. Bring to a boil over high heat. Reduce heat to low. Cover; simmer 1½ to 2 hours until beef is very tender.

3. Using 2 forks, pull beef into coarse shreds in skillet. Increase heat to medium. Cook, uncovered, 10 to 15 minutes until most of liquid has evaporated. Keep warm.

4. Heat 4 to 5 inches of oil in deep fat fryer or deep saucepan over medium-high heat to 375°F; adjust heat to maintain temperature. For taco shells, place 1 tortilla in taco fryer basket;** close gently. Fry tortilla ½ to 1 minute until crisp and golden. Open basket; gently remove taco shell. Drain on paper towels. Repeat with remaining tortillas.

5. Layer beef, cheese, lettuce and tomato in each taco shell. Garnish, if desired.   *Makes 6 servings*

**Taco fryer baskets are available in large supermarkets and in housewares stores.

Spicy Beef Tacos

86 Stuffed Tortillas

Tex-Mex Dinners

GRILLED CHICKEN ADOBO

½ cup chopped onion
⅓ cup lime juice
6 cloves garlic, coarsely chopped
1 teaspoon dried oregano leaves
1 teaspoon ground cumin
½ teaspoon dried thyme leaves
¼ teaspoon ground red pepper
6 boneless skinless chicken breasts
3 tablespoons chopped fresh cilantro

1. Combine onion, lime juice and garlic in food processor. Process until onion is finely minced. Transfer to resealable plastic food storage bag. Add oregano, cumin, thyme and red pepper; knead bag until blended. Place chicken in bag; press out air and seal. Turn to coat chicken with marinade. Refrigerate 30 minutes or up to 4 hours.

2. Spray grid with nonstick cooking spray. Prepare grill for direct cooking. Remove chicken from marinade; discard marinade. Place chicken on grid 3 to 4 inches from medium-hot coals. Grill 5 to 7 minutes on each side or until chicken is no longer pink in center. Transfer to clean serving platter and sprinkle with cilantro. *Makes 6 servings*

GRILLED CHICKEN ADOBO

Chicken Casserole Olé

12 boneless, skinless chicken tenders
2 cups water
1 can (15 ounces) mild chili beans, undrained
1 cup salsa
½ cup chopped green bell pepper
2 cups UNCLE BEN'S® Instant Rice
2 cups (8 ounces) shredded Mexican cheese blend, divided
2 cups bite-size tortilla chips

1. Spray large skillet with nonstick cooking spray. Add chicken; cook over medium-high heat 12 to 15 minutes or until lightly browned on both sides and chicken is no longer pink in center.

2. Add water, beans with liquid, salsa and bell pepper. Bring to a boil; add rice and 1 cup cheese. Cover; remove from heat and let stand 5 minutes or until liquid is absorbed. Top with tortilla chips and remaining 1 cup cheese; let stand, covered, 3 to 5 minutes or until cheese is melted.   *Makes 6 servings*

Chicken Casserole Olé

BEEF MOLE TAMALE PIE

1½ pounds ground beef chuck
1 medium onion, chopped
1 green bell pepper, chopped
2 cloves garlic, minced
1 package (10 ounces) frozen whole kernel corn,
    partially thawed
1¼ cups medium-hot salsa
1 tablespoon unsweetened cocoa powder
2 teaspoons ground cumin
1½ teaspoons salt, divided
1 teaspoon dried oregano leaves
¼ teaspoon ground cinnamon
2 cups (8 ounces) shredded Monterey Jack
    or Cheddar cheese
⅓ cup chopped fresh cilantro
1 cup all-purpose flour
¾ cup yellow cornmeal
3 tablespoons sugar
2 teaspoons baking powder
⅔ cup milk
3 tablespoons butter, melted
1 egg, beaten
    Cilantro leaves, chili pepper and sour cream for garnish
    (optional)

1. Preheat oven to 400°F. Spray 11×7-inch baking dish with nonstick cooking spray.

2. Brown beef with onion, bell pepper and garlic in large deep skillet or Dutch oven over medium heat. Pour off drippings. Stir in corn, salsa, cocoa, cumin, 1 teaspoon salt, oregano and cinnamon. Bring to a boil. Reduce heat to medium-low; simmer, uncovered, 8 minutes, stirring occasionally. Remove from heat; stir in cheese and cilantro. Spread in prepared dish.

continued on page 94

BEEF MOLE TAMALE PIE

Beef Mole Tamale Pie, continued

3. Combine flour, cornmeal, sugar, baking powder and remaining ½ teaspoon salt in large bowl. Add milk, butter and egg; stir just until dry ingredients are moistened. Spread batter evenly over meat mixture.

4. Bake 15 minutes. *Reduce oven temperature to 350°F.* Bake 20 minutes or until topping is light brown and filling is bubbly. Let stand 5 minutes before serving. Garnish, if desired.

Makes 6 servings

TEXAS RANCH CHILI BEANS

1 pound lean ground beef

1 can (28 ounces) whole peeled tomatoes, undrained

2 cans (15½ ounces each) chili beans

1 cup chopped onions

1 cup water

1 packet (1 ounce) HIDDEN VALLEY® The Original Ranch® Salad Dressing & Seasoning Mix

1 teaspoon chili powder

1 bay leaf

In Dutch oven, brown beef over medium-high heat; drain off fat. Add tomatoes, breaking up with spoon. Stir in beans, onions, water, salad dressing & seasoning mix, chili powder and bay leaf. Bring to boil; reduce heat and simmer, uncovered, 1 hour, stirring occasionally. Remove bay leaf just before serving.

Makes 8 servings

BREAKFAST MIGAS

1 tablespoon olive oil
1 small onion, chopped
1 jalapeño pepper,* seeded and diced
3 corn tortillas, cut into 1-inch pieces
1 medium tomato, seeded and diced
6 eggs
2 tablespoons chunky salsa
1 cup (4 ounces) shredded Monterey Jack cheese
1 small ripe avocado, peeled and diced
1 tablespoon lime juice
   Sour cream
   Chopped fresh cilantro

*Jalapeño peppers can sting and irritate the skin; wear rubber gloves when handling peppers and do not touch eyes. Wash hands after handling.

1. Heat olive oil in 12-inch nonstick skillet over medium heat. Add onion and jalapeño pepper; cook and stir 1 minute or until soft.

2. Add tortillas and tomato; cook about 2 minutes or until soft and heated through.

3. Slightly beat eggs and salsa in small bowl; add to skillet. Cook, stirring occasionally, until eggs are firmly scrambled.

4. Remove skillet from heat; stir in cheese. Garnish each serving with avocado tossed in lime juice, sour cream and cilantro. *Makes 6 servings*

NOTE: Migas, a Mexican breakfast dish, is traditionally made in a skillet with leftover, stale tortillas that are torn by hand into small pieces.

Turkey Cutlets with Chipotle Pepper Mole

1 package BUTTERBALL® Fresh Boneless
    Turkey Breast Cutlets
1 can (14½ ounces) chicken broth
¼ cup raisins
4 cloves garlic, minced
1 chipotle chile pepper in adobo sauce
2 tablespoons ground almonds
2 teaspoons unsweetened cocoa
½ cup chopped fresh cilantro
2 tablespoons fresh lime juice
½ teaspoon salt

To prepare chipotle sauce, combine chicken broth, raisins, garlic, chile pepper, almonds and cocoa in medium saucepan. Simmer over low heat 10 minutes. Pour into food processor or blender; process until smooth. Add cilantro, lime juice and salt. Grill cutlets according to package directions. Serve chipotle sauce over grilled cutlets with Mexican polenta.*

Makes 7 servings

*To make Mexican polenta, cook 1 cup instant cornmeal polenta according to package directions. Stir in ½ teaspoon garlic powder, ½ teaspoon salt and 2 cups taco-seasoned cheese.

PREP TIME: 20 minutes

tip Moles are complex sauces often reddish-brown in color. The many variations contain chiles, herbs, spices, nuts, ground seeds and often a small amount of chocolate. The sauces are generally smooth in texture and frequently served with poultry.

TURKEY CUTLET WITH CHIPOTLE PEPPER MOLE

Rawhide Strips with Flame Sauce

2 tablespoons vegetable oil
2 teaspoons ground cumin
2 teaspoons chili powder
2 teaspoons brown sugar
2 teaspoons minced garlic
1 teaspoon salt
¼ teaspoon ground red pepper
2 pounds skirt steak, cut into 6-inch pieces
Flame Sauce* (page 100)
Flour tortillas (optional)

*If desired, use prepared hot salsa in place of Flame Sauce.

1. Combine oil, cumin, chili powder, brown sugar, garlic, salt and red pepper in small bowl. Rub mixture on both sides of steak. Refrigerate steaks 2 hours.

2. Prepare Flame Sauce. Preheat broiler.

3. Place steaks on rack of broiler pan, 4 inches from heat. Broil steaks 4 to 6 minutes per side or until well browned outside and rare to medium doneness inside. Cut across the grain into thin strips. Serve with Flame Sauce and flour tortillas, if desired. *Makes 8 to 10 servings*

Rawhide Strips with Flame Sauce

FLAME SAUCE

4 cups chopped tomatoes
¼ cup minced red onion
1 clove garlic, minced
1 teaspoon minced habanero chile pepper*
¼ cup chopped fresh cilantro
1 tablespoon fresh lime juice
½ teaspoon salt
¼ teaspoon pepper
¼ teaspoon ground cumin

*Habanero peppers can sting and irritate the skin; wear rubber gloves when handling peppers and do not touch eyes. Wash hands after handling.

Combine tomatoes, onion, garlic and chile in large bowl; drain excess liquid. Stir in cilantro, lime juice, salt, pepper and cumin. *Makes about 3 cups*

CHILI BEEF MAC

1 pound lean ground beef or ground turkey
4 teaspoons Mexican seasoning*
⅔ cup milk
1 (4.8-ounce) package PASTA RONI® Four Cheese Flavor with Corkscrew Pasta
1 medium green, red or yellow bell pepper, diced
½ cup salsa
¼ cup chopped fresh cilantro or sliced green onions

*2 teaspoons chili powder, 1 teaspoon ground cumin and 1 teaspoon garlic salt can be substituted.

1. In large skillet over medium-high heat, cook ground beef and Mexican seasoning for 5 minutes, stirring occasionally.

2. Add 1¼ cups water, milk, pasta, bell pepper, salsa and Special Seasonings. Bring to a boil. Reduce heat to low. Cover; simmer 8 to 9 minutes or until pasta is tender. Stir in cilantro. Let stand 5 minutes before serving. *Makes 4 servings*

CHILAQUILES

2 tablespoons vegetable oil

1 medium onion, chopped

1 package (1.0 ounce) LAWRY'S® Taco Spices
    & Seasonings

1 can (28 ounces) diced tomatoes, in juice

1 can (4 ounces) diced green chiles (optional)

6 ounces plain tortilla chips

4 cups shredded Monterey Jack cheese (about 16 ounces)

1 cup (8 ounces) sour cream

½ cup shredded cheddar cheese (about 2 ounces)

In large skillet, heat oil over medium high heat. Add onion
and cook until tender. Add Taco Spices & Seasonings,
tomatoes and chiles; mix well. Bring to a boil; reduce heat
to low and cook, uncovered, 10 minutes, stirring occasionally.
Spray 2-quart casserole dish with nonstick cooking spray;
arrange ½ of tortilla chips, sauce and Monterey Jack cheese.
Repeat layers; top with sour cream. Bake in 350°F oven for
25 minutes. Sprinkle with cheddar cheese and bake 5 minutes
longer. Let stand 10 minutes before serving.

Makes 6 servings

MEAL IDEA: Serve with a marinated vegetable salad and fresh
fruit.

PREP TIME: 15 minutes
COOK TIME: 45 minutes

Salsa Chicken Fajitas

> 2 tablespoons vegetable oil
> 1 medium onion, sliced
> 1 medium red bell pepper, cut into ¼-inch strips
> 1 medium green bell pepper, cut into ¼-inch strips
> 1 clove garlic, minced
> 4 boneless skinless chicken breasts (about 1 pound), cut into ¼-inch strips
> ½ cup chunky salsa
> 1 tablespoon minced jalapeño pepper*
> Salt and black pepper
> 8 (8-inch) flour tortillas
> Guacamole
> Shredded mozzarella or Monterey Jack cheese
> Additional chunky salsa

*Jalapeño peppers can sting and irritate the skin; wear rubber gloves when handling peppers and do not touch eyes. Wash hands after handling.

1. Heat oil in large skillet over medium-high heat. Add onion, bell peppers and garlic. Cook and stir 3 to 4 minutes or until crisp-tender. Remove vegetables with slotted spoon; set aside.

2. Add chicken to skillet. Cook and stir 4 minutes or until chicken is no longer pink in center. Return vegetables to skillet. Add salsa and jalapeño. Season with salt and black pepper to taste; cover. Continue cooking 2 minutes or until thoroughly heated.

3. Meanwhile, stack tortillas and wrap in foil. Heat tortillas in 350°F oven 10 minutes or until warm. Fill tortillas with guacamole, chicken mixture and cheese; top with additional salsa. *Makes 4 servings*

Salsa Chicken Fajitas

Fiery Chili Beef

1 to 2 beef flank steaks (1 to 1½ pounds)
1 can (28 ounces) diced tomatoes, undrained
1 can (15 ounces) pinto beans, rinsed and drained
1 medium onion, chopped
2 cloves garlic, minced
½ teaspoon salt
½ teaspoon ground cumin
¼ teaspoon black pepper
1 canned chipotle chile pepper in adobo sauce
1 teaspoon adobo sauce from canned chile pepper
   Flour tortillas

Slow Cooker Directions

1. Cut flank steak into 6 evenly-sized pieces. Combine flank steak, tomatoes with juice, beans, onion, garlic, salt, cumin and black pepper in slow cooker.

2. Dice chile pepper. Add pepper and adobo sauce to slow cooker; mix well.

3. Cover; cook on LOW 7 to 8 hours. Serve with tortillas.

Makes 6 servings

Note: Chipotle chile peppers are dried, smoked jalapeño peppers with a very hot yet smoky, sweet flavor. They can be found dried, pickled and canned in adobo sauce.

Prep Time: 15 minutes
Cook Time: 7 to 8 hours (LOW)

Fiery Chili Beef

SPICY CHICKEN CASSEROLE WITH CORNBREAD

2 tablespoons olive oil

4 boneless skinless chicken breasts, cut into bite-size pieces

1 envelope (about 1 ounce) taco seasoning

1 can (about 15 ounces) black beans, rinsed and drained

1 can (14½ ounces) diced tomatoes, drained

1 can (about 10 ounces) Mexican-style corn, drained

1 can (about 4 ounces) diced green chilies, drained

½ cup mild salsa

1 box (about 8½ ounces) cornbread mix, plus ingredients to prepare

½ cup (2 ounces) shredded Cheddar cheese

¼ cup chopped red bell pepper

1. Preheat oven to 350°F. Spray 2-quart casserole with nonstick cooking spray. Set aside. Heat oil in large skillet over medium heat. Cook chicken until no longer pink.

2. Sprinkle taco seasoning over chicken. Add black beans, tomatoes, corn, chilies and salsa; stir until well blended. Transfer to prepared dish.

3. Prepare cornbread mix according to package directions, adding cheese and bell pepper. Spread batter over chicken mixture.

4. Bake 30 minutes or until cornbread is golden brown.

Makes 4 to 6 servings

SPICY CHICKEN CASSEROLE WITH CORNBREAD

Fabulous Fajitas

½ cup (1 stick) unsalted butter, melted, divided

4 cups julienned onions

2 cups julienned red, green or yellow bell peppers

4 boneless beef sirloin strip steaks (10½ ounces each), trimmed and cut into julienned strips

2 tablespoons Chef Paul Prudhomme's Meat Magic®, divided

½ cup freshly squeezed lime juice

Flour tortillas, warmed

Sour cream

Guacamole

Tomato salsa

Shredded lettuce

In 12-inch heavy skillet, heat 4 tablespoons butter over medium-high heat. Add onions; sauté until onions are clear and turning brown on edges, about 3 minutes, stirring occasionally. Add bell peppers. Sauté until onions are soft and bell peppers are still crispy, about 3 minutes more. Transfer vegetables to plate; set skillet aside.

Heat several sizzle platters or large cast-iron skillet in 400°F oven.

Meanwhile, place meat strips in large bowl; sprinkle with 1 tablespoon plus 1 teaspoon Meat Magic®, tossing to coat well. Pour lime juice over meat and toss again. Marinate at least 10 to 15 minutes, tossing occasionally.

Heat reserved skillet over medium-high heat, 40 to 45 seconds; add remaining butter (it will sizzle). Drain meat; reserve marinade. Add meat to skillet. Cook about 45 seconds, turning meat frequently to coat with butter. Add reserved vegetables; sauté about 15 seconds, tossing constantly to combine. Add reserved marinade; sprinkle with remaining 2 teaspoons Meat Magic®; cook about 1 minute more, stirring well. Remove from heat; pour onto heated sizzle platters. Serve hot with traditional condiments.   *Makes 6 to 8 servings*

Fabulous Fajitas

JALAPEÑO-LIME CHICKEN

1 tablespoon olive oil
1 tablespoon lime juice
1 jalapeño pepper,* seeded and diced
1 teaspoon cumin
1 teaspoon lime zest
2 cloves garlic, minced
¼ teaspoon salt
1 pound boneless skinless chicken breasts
　 Sliced jalapeño peppers* and black olives

*Jalapeño peppers can sting and irritate the skin; wear rubber gloves when handling peppers and do not touch eyes. Wash hands after handling.

1. Combine oil, lime juice, jalapeño, cumin, lime zest, garlic and salt in small bowl. Brush mixture on both sides of chicken using a pastry brush. Cover with plastic wrap; marinate in refrigerator 30 minutes or up to 8 hours.

2. Preheat grill to medium-high. Grill chicken 5 to 6 minutes on each side or until no longer pink in center. Garnish with jalapeños and black olives. *Makes 4 servings*

CARNITAS

2 to 2½ pounds fresh pork butt roast
2 bay leaves
2 cloves garlic, minced
1 teaspoon chili powder
¾ teaspoon salt
½ teaspoon black pepper
½ teaspoon dried oregano leaves
½ teaspoon ground cumin
½ cup water
Guacamole (recipe follows) *or* 2 cups salsa

Preheat oven to 350°F. Trim external fat from meat; cut meat into 1-inch cubes. Combine bay leaves, garlic, chili powder, salt, pepper, oregano and cumin in large shallow roasting pan (pan should be large enough to hold meat in single layer). Gradually add water; mix well. Place meat in pan; stir until well coated. Cover with foil. Bake 45 minutes. Remove foil; continue baking 45 to 60 minutes or until most of the liquid has evaporated and meat begins to brown. Discard bay leaves. Transfer meat to fondue pot or chafing dish; keep warm. Serve with Guacamole. *Makes 12 to 14 servings*

GUACAMOLE

2 large avocados, peeled and pitted
¼ cup finely chopped tomato
2 tablespoons lime juice or lemon juice
2 tablespoons grated onion with juice
½ teaspoon salt
¼ teaspoon hot pepper sauce
Black pepper

Place avocados in medium bowl; mash coarsely with fork. Stir in tomato, lime juice, onion, salt and pepper sauce; mix well. Add black pepper to taste. Serve immediately or cover and refrigerate up to 2 hours. *Makes 2 cups*

SOUTHWESTERN CHILIES RELLENOS

2 tablespoons olive oil

½ teaspoon white pepper

½ teaspoon salt

½ teaspoon ground red pepper

¼ teaspoon ground cloves

4 cans (4 ounces each) whole green chilies, drained, seeded

1½ cups (6 ounces) shredded Wisconsin Cheddar cheese

1½ cups (6 ounces) shredded Wisconsin Monterey Jack cheese

1 package (16 ounces) egg roll wrappers

1 egg yolk plus 1 teaspoon water

Vegetable oil

Combine olive oil and seasonings in small bowl. Add chilies; toss to coat. Let stand 1 hour. Combine cheeses in separate small bowl.

For each chili relleno, place 1 chili in center of 1 egg roll wrapper; top with ¼ cup cheese mixture. Brush edges of egg roll wrapper with combined egg yolk and water. Fold lengthwise edges over filling, overlapping edges; press together. Seal ends, enclosing filling.

Heat vegetable oil in heavy saucepan over medium-high heat until oil reaches 375°F; adjust heat to maintain temperature. Fry chilies rellenos, a few at a time, in hot oil 2 to 3 minutes or until golden brown. Drain on paper towels.

Makes 6 servings

*Favorite recipe from **Wisconsin Milk Marketing Board***

STUFFED PORK TENDERLOIN WITH CILANTRO-LIME PESTO

1 to 1½ pounds pork tenderloin

3 large cloves garlic, peeled

½ onion, cut into chunks

½ cup lightly packed fresh cilantro

2 tablespoons lime juice

1 teaspoon ORTEGA® Diced Jalapeños

2 tablespoons corn oil

½ cup (2 ounces) shredded Monterey Jack
   or crumbled Cotija cheese

ORTEGA Salsa

PREHEAT oven to 400°F.

CUT tenderloin lengthwise almost in half. Open; lay flat between two pieces of waxed paper. Pound with meat mallet or rolling pin to ½-inch thickness.

PLACE garlic, onion, cilantro, lime juice and jalapeños in food processor or blender container; cover. Process until coarsely chopped. Process, while slowly adding oil, for 10 to 15 seconds or until mixture is almost smooth. Spread half of cilantro mixture over tenderloin; top with cheese. Roll up; tie with cotton string. Spread remaining cilantro mixture over top. Place on rack in roasting pan.

BAKE for 55 to 60 minutes or until internal temperature of 160°F is reached. Cool in pan on wire rack for 5 minutes. Remove string; slice. Serve with salsa.   *Makes 4 servings*

TIP: Ladle ORTEGA Thick & Chunky Salsa onto bottom of plate and top with tenderloin slices for a fantastic presentation!

*STUFFED PORK TENDERLOIN
WITH CILANTRO-LIME PESTO*

CHICKEN FAJITAS

4 boneless skinless chicken breast halves
    (about 1½ pounds)
¼ cup orange juice
2 tablespoons lime juice
2 tablespoons lemon juice
1 clove garlic, minced
1 teaspoon chili powder
½ teaspoon salt
1 tablespoon vegetable oil
1 medium red bell pepper, cut into strips
1 medium green bell pepper, cut into strips
1 medium yellow bell pepper, cut into strips
1 medium onion, sliced
10 flour tortillas, warmed
1 cup sour cream
1 cup salsa
1 can (2¼ ounces) sliced black olives, drained

Combine orange juice, lime juice, lemon juice and garlic in large bowl. Season chicken with chili powder and salt. Place chicken in juice mixture, turning to coat. Cover; marinate in refrigerator 30 minutes. Remove chicken. Place marinade in small saucepan. Bring to a boil over medium-high heat; keep warm. Place chicken on broiler rack or grill about 6 inches from heat. Broil or grill, turning and basting with marinade, 10 minutes or until no longer pink in center. Heat oil in large skillet over medium-high heat until hot. Add peppers and onion; cook and stir about 5 minutes or until onion is tender. Slice chicken into strips; add to pepper-onion mixture. Divide chicken-pepper mixture evenly in centers of tortillas. Roll up tortillas; top each with dollop of sour cream, salsa and olives.

Makes 5 servings (2 fajitas each)

*Favorite recipe from **National Chicken Council***

CHICKEN FAJITAS

PORK TENDERLOIN MOLE

1½ pounds pork tenderloin (about 2 whole)
1 teaspoon vegetable oil
½ cup chopped onion
1 clove garlic, minced
1 cup Mexican-style chili beans, undrained
¼ cup chili sauce
¼ cup raisins
2 tablespoons water
1 tablespoon peanut butter
1 teaspoon unsweetened cocoa
   Dash each salt, ground cinnamon and ground cloves

Place tenderloin in shallow baking pan. Roast at 350°F for 30 minutes or until juicy and slightly pink in center.

Heat oil in medium saucepan. Cook onion and garlic over low heat for 5 minutes. Combine onion and garlic with remaining ingredients in food processor; process until almost smooth. Heat mixture in saucepan thoroughly over low temperature, stirring frequently. Serve over tenderloin slices.

Makes 6 servings

Favorite recipe from **National Pork Board**

tip Quick-cooking pork tenderloin is an ideal choice for easy entertaining. This delicate, lean meat should be cooked just until it is barely pink in the center. Overcooking causes pork tenderloin to become dry.

TURKEY CUTLETS WITH TEX-MEX SALSA

1 package BUTTERBALL® Fresh Boneless
   Turkey Breast Cutlets
1 can (15 ounces) black beans, rinsed and drained
1 can (11 ounces) Mexican-style corn, drained
1 cup salsa
2 tablespoons chopped fresh cilantro
1 tablespoon Mexican seasoning blend*
1 teaspoon salt
1 tablespoon vegetable oil
   Lime wedges (optional)

*To make your own Mexican seasoning, combine 1½ teaspoons chili powder, ¾ teaspoon oregano and ¾ teaspoon cumin.

Combine black beans, corn, salsa and cilantro in large bowl; stir to blend. Chill until served. Combine seasoning blend and salt. Dip cutlets into seasoning mixture. Heat oil in large skillet over medium heat until hot. Cook cutlets 2 to 2½ minutes on each side until lightly browned and no longer pink. Place bean salsa on serving platter; arrange cutlets on top of salsa. Serve with a squeeze of fresh lime. *Makes 7 servings*

PREP TIME: 30 minutes

SOUTHWESTERN TORTILLA STACK

    1 (30-ounce) can vegetarian refried beans
    ½ cup sour cream
    1 (4-ounce) can chopped green chilies, drained
    ½ teaspoon ground cumin
    3 (10-inch) flour tortillas
    1 cup (4 ounces) shredded Cheddar cheese

1. Preheat oven to 425°F. Grease 10-inch round casserole dish.

2. Combine beans, sour cream, chilies and cumin; set aside.

3. Place one tortilla in bottom of prepared casserole. Top with half of the bean mixture and one third of the cheese. Top with second tortilla; repeat layers of beans and cheese.

4. Cover with remaining tortilla; sprinkle with remaining cheese. Cover with foil.

5. Bake 20 minutes or until thoroughly heated. Cut into wedges. Serve with salsa, if desired.   *Makes 4 to 6 servings*

Salads & Sides

ADOBE SUMMER SALAD

3 cups cooked white rice, chilled
2 cups diced red and/or yellow or orange bell peppers
1 can (about 15 ounces) black beans, rinsed and drained
1 large tomato, chopped
1 cup diced jicama
1 cup diced cooked chicken or turkey breast
¾ cup sliced green onions
¼ cup chopped fresh cilantro
1 cup thick and chunky salsa
2 tablespoons fresh lime juice
2 tablespoons vegetable oil
¼ teaspoon salt
8 large romaine lettuce leaves
Lime wedges (optional)

1. Combine rice, bell peppers, beans, tomato, jicama, chicken, green onions and cilantro in large bowl; mix well.

2. Combine salsa, lime juice, oil and salt in small bowl. Add to salad; toss well. (Salad may be served immediately or covered and chilled up to 8 hours before serving.) Serve salad over lettuce leaves with lime wedges. *Makes 6 servings*

ADOBE SUMMER SALAD

Southwestern Chicken Salad

1 package (1.27 ounces) LAWRY'S® Spices & Seasonings
   for Fajitas
3 tablespoons vegetable oil
2½ tablespoons lime juice
1½ teaspoons LAWRY'S® Garlic Powder With Parsley
6 boneless, skinless chicken breasts (about 1½ pounds)
6 cups torn lettuce
½ red onion, thinly sliced
1 large tomato, cut into wedges
1 avocado, thinly sliced
   WISH-BONE® Ranch Dressing

In small bowl, mix together Spices & Seasonings for Fajitas,
oil, lime juice and Garlic Powder With Parsley. Place chicken in
large Ziploc® Brand Bag. Pour on fajitas-marinade mixture; seal
bag and toss to coat chicken. Refrigerate for 30 minutes to
overnight. Remove chicken from bag; discarding marinade.
Grill or broil chicken 15 minutes or until thoroughly cooked.
Let cool slightly, slice thinly or cut into cubes. To arrange
salads, place chicken on beds of lettuce. Top each with equal
portions of onion, tomato and avocado. Drizzle with ranch
dressing. *Makes 4 to 6 servings*

PREP TIME: 15 minutes
MARINATE TIME: 30 minutes
COOK TIME: 15 minutes

tip This grilled marinated chicken is also excellent for
sandwiches. What could be better than thinly sliced
grilled chicken served in a lettuce-lined crusty roll along with
sliced avocados and tomatoes? Drizzle with a small amount of
dressing for a fabulous gourmet sandwich.

SOUTHWESTERN CHICKEN SALAD

ARROZ ROJOS

  2 tablespoons vegetable oil
  1 cup uncooked long-grain white rice (not converted)
  ½ cup finely chopped white onion
  1 clove garlic, minced
  ½ teaspoon salt
  ½ teaspoon ground cumin
    Dash chili powder
  2 large tomatoes, peeled, seeded and chopped
1½ cups chicken broth
  ⅓ cup shelled fresh or thawed frozen peas
  2 tablespoons chopped pimiento

1. Heat oil in medium skillet over medium heat until hot. Add rice. Cook and stir 2 minutes or until rice turns opaque.

2. Add onion; cook and stir 1 minute. Stir in garlic, salt, cumin and chili powder. Add tomatoes; cook and stir 2 minutes.

3. Stir in broth. Bring to a boil over high heat. Reduce heat to low. Cover and simmer 15 minutes or until rice is almost tender.

4. Stir in peas and pimiento. Cover; cook 2 to 4 minutes until rice is tender and all liquid has been absorbed. Rice grains will be slightly firm and separate, rather than soft and sticky.

Makes 4 to 6 servings

Salsa Beef Salad

1 pound ground beef
1 can (15½ ounces) pinto beans, rinsed and drained
2 jalapeño peppers,* seeded and chopped
2 tablespoons chili powder
½ teaspoon ground cumin
   Salt and black pepper
1 head iceberg lettuce, shredded
2 medium tomatoes, diced
½ cup shredded Pepper Jack cheese
¼ cup chopped fresh cilantro
½ cup chopped green onions
1 cup salsa
   Juice of 1 lime
1 package (12 ounces) corn tortilla chips, broken
   Sour cream (optional)

*Jalapeño peppers can sting and irritate the skin; wear rubber gloves when handling peppers and do not touch eyes. Wash hands after handling

1. Brown ground beef in large skillet over medium-high heat, stirring to separate meat. Drain and discard fat. Add beans, jalapeños, chili powder and cumin; season with salt and pepper. Cook and stir 15 minutes. Set aside to cool.

2. Toss together lettuce, tomatoes, cheese and cilantro in large salad bowl. Top with ground beef mixture, green onions, salsa and lime juice. Sprinkle with corn chips. Serve with sour cream, if desired. *Makes 4 to 6 servings*

Salsa Beef Salad

COLACHE

2 tablespoons vegetable oil

1 butternut squash (about 2 pounds), peeled, seeded and diced

1 medium onion, coarsely chopped

1 clove garlic, minced

1 can (14½ ounces) diced tomatoes, undrained

1 green bell pepper, seeded and cut into 1-inch pieces

1 can (14½ ounces) whole kernel corn, drained

1 canned green chile, coarsely chopped (optional)

½ teaspoon salt

¼ teaspoon black pepper

1. Heat oil in large skillet over medium heat. Add squash, onion and garlic; cook 5 minutes or until onion is tender. Add tomatoes with juice and bell pepper to skillet. Bring to a boil over high heat. Cover; reduce heat and simmer 15 minutes.

2. Add corn, chile, if desired, salt and pepper. Simmer, covered, 5 minutes or until squash is tender. Uncover; increase heat to high. Continue cooking a few minutes or until most of liquid has evaporated. *Makes 6 to 8 servings*

RICE CHILI VERDE

1 tablespoon butter
¼ cup finely chopped onion
1 cup small-curd cottage cheese
1 cup (½ pint) sour cream
½ teaspoon salt
⅛ teaspoon white pepper
1 can (7 ounces) whole green chilies, drained and cut
    into 1-inch pieces
3 cups cooked rice
1 cup (4 ounces) shredded Monterey Jack cheese
1 cup (4 ounces) shredded Cheddar cheese

1. Preheat oven to 350°F. Butter 1½-quart casserole.

2. Melt butter in small skillet over medium heat. Add onion; cook until tender. Combine onion, cottage cheese, sour cream, salt and pepper in medium bowl; mix well. Stir in chilies.

3. Spoon half of rice into prepared casserole; cover with half of cottage cheese mixture. Top with half of Monterey Jack cheese and half of Cheddar cheese. Repeat layers with remaining ingredients. Bake 25 to 30 minutes or until rice is hot and cheese is melted. *Makes 6 servings*

tip To cook rice, bring 2 cups water and 1 teaspoon salt to a boil in a medium saucepan over medium-high heat. Slowly add 1 cup long-grain rice so that the water continues to boil. Stir briefly. Reduce heat to low. Cover and cook for 18 minutes or until the rice is tender. Remove saucepan from the heat and let stand, covered, for 5 minutes. Fluff rice with a fork.

FRIJOLES

1 pound uncooked dried pinto, pink, red or black beans
  Cold water
½ cup (¼ pound) finely diced salt pork *or* 2 tablespoons
  bacon drippings
8 cups water
1 small onion, finely chopped
1 clove garlic, minced
  Salt

1. Sort beans, discarding any foreign material. Place beans in large Dutch oven. Add enough cold water to cover beans by 2 inches. Cover. Bring to a boil over high heat. Boil 2 minutes. Remove from heat; let soak, covered, 1 hour. Drain.

2. Cook pork in small skillet until fat begins to melt. Add pork and drippings to beans. Add 8 cups water, onion and garlic. Simmer, partially covered, until beans are tender, 1½ to 2 hours for pinto, pink or red beans, 2½ hours for black beans. To reduce liquid, uncover and boil over medium heat until desired consistency, stirring more frequently as mixture thickens. Season to taste with salt.   *Makes 6 to 8 servings*

FIESTA BEANS: Follow directions for Frijoles but use 1½ pounds ham shank in place of salt pork. When beans are cooked, remove meat; cut into bite-size pieces, discarding bone. Stir meat into beans; heat to simmering.

REFRIED BEANS: Remove 4 cups Frijoles with slotted spoon. Mash beans with potato masher or process in blender or food processor container fitted with metal blade until coarsely mashed. Heat 2 tablespoons bacon drippings in large skillet. Add mashed beans. Cook over medium heat until thick and bubbly. Top with 1 cup (4 ounces) shredded Cheddar or Colby cheese. Let cheese melt before serving.

MEXICAN SLAW

1 corn tortilla, cut into thin strips
Nonstick cooking spray
¼ teaspoon chili powder
3 cups shredded green cabbage
1 cup shredded red cabbage
½ cup shredded carrots
½ cup sliced radishes
½ cup corn kernels
¼ cup coarsely chopped cilantro
¼ cup mayonnaise
1 tablespoon lime juice
2 teaspoons vinegar
1 teaspoon honey
½ teaspoon cumin
¼ teaspoon salt
¼ teaspoon black pepper

1. Preheat oven to 350°F. Arrange tortilla strips in even layer on nonstick baking sheet. Spray strips with cooking spray and sprinkle with chili powder. Bake 6 to 8 minutes or until strips are crisp. Remove from oven and set aside.

2. Combine remaining ingredients in a large bowl; mix well. To serve, place equal amounts of slaw on serving plates and top with baked tortilla strips. *Makes 8 servings*

JICAMA SALAD

1 cucumber
1 small jicama
½ red bell pepper, cut into 1-inch strips
½ green bell pepper, cut into 1-inch strips
½ small onion, thinly sliced crosswise
¼ cup olive oil
3 tablespoons lime juice
½ teaspoon dried oregano
¼ teaspoon salt
¼ teaspoon chili powder
⅛ teaspoon black pepper

1. Peel cucumber; cut in half lengthwise. Scoop out and discard seeds; cut crosswise into ¼-inch slices. Place in large bowl. Peel jicama; cut into ¼-inch slices, then cut slices into matchstick-size pieces. Add to cucumber. Add bell peppers and onion.

2. Whisk oil, lime juice, oregano, salt, chili powder and black pepper in small bowl until well blended. Pour over salad; toss until vegetables are evenly coated.

3. Place salad in serving bowl. Serve immediately or cover and refrigerate up to 4 hours.   *Makes 6 servings*

tip Jicama is a large, round root vegetable with a rough brown skin. The white flesh has a sweet flavor and crunchy texture. Peel the skin before cutting the crisp, slightly sweet flesh into matchstick-size pieces or slices. Jicama is most often eaten raw. It can be served with dips, added to salads or served as an appetizer with ground chiles and lime juice.

Fajita Nacho Salad

1 pork tenderloin or ¾ pound beef top sirloin steak,
    cut into bite-size strips
¾ to 1 cup salsa, divided
1 cup sliced red onion
1 cup julienne-sliced DOLE® Red or Yellow Bell Pepper
1 package (10 ounces) DOLE® Organic Salad Blend
    Romaine Hearts & Radicchio or Baby Spinach Salad
1 cup shredded cheddar cheese
    Blue corn chips or corn tortilla chips
    Avocado slices (optional)

■ Cook pork in 2 tablespoons salsa in non-stick skillet for
3 minutes or until meat is no longer pink. Remove from skillet;
drain well. Add more salsa, if necessary; stir-fry onions and bell
peppers for 3 minutes; remove from heat and drain.

■ Toss together salad blend, pork, vegetables, cheese and
remaining salsa in bowl.

■ Arrange layer of corn chips on serving platter. Spoon salad
over chips. Garnish with avocado slices, if desired.

Makes 3 to 4 servings

PREP TIME: 20 minutes
COOK TIME: 6 minutes

Salads & Sides

SOUTHWESTERN CORN AND BEANS

1 tablespoon olive oil
1 large onion, diced
1 or 2 jalapeño peppers,* diced
1 clove garlic, minced
2 cans (15 ounces each) light red kidney beans, rinsed
　　and drained
1 bag (16 ounces) frozen corn, thawed
1 can (14½ ounces) diced tomatoes, undrained
1 green bell pepper, cut into 1-inch pieces
2 teaspoons medium-hot chili powder
¾ teaspoon salt
½ teaspoon ground cumin
½ teaspoon black pepper
　　Sour cream or plain yogurt (optional)
　　Sliced black olives (optional)

*Jalapeño peppers can sting and irritate the skin; wear rubber gloves when handling peppers and do not touch eyes. Wash hands after handling.

SLOW COOKER DIRECTIONS

1. Heat oil in medium skillet over medium heat. Add onion, jalapeño and garlic; cook 5 minutes. Combine onion mixture, beans, corn, tomatoes with juice, bell pepper, chili powder, salt, cumin and black pepper in slow cooker; mix well.

2. Cover; cook on LOW 7 to 8 hours or on HIGH 2 to 3 hours.

3. Serve with sour cream and black olives, if desired.

Makes 6 servings

PREP TIME: 15 minutes
COOK TIME: 7 to 8 hours (LOW) • 2 to 3 hours (HIGH)

SOUTHWESTERN CORN AND BEANS

STUFFED CHAYOTES

2 large chayotes, cut in half lengthwise
2 tablespoons butter
½ cup chopped onion
1 clove garlic, minced
1 large tomato, peeled, seeded and chopped
2 tablespoons chopped fresh parsley
½ cup cooked whole kernel corn
½ teaspoon salt
⅛ teaspoon black pepper
½ cup (2 ounces) shredded Cheddar cheese

1. Cook chayote halves in 1 inch boiling water in large covered skillet 20 to 25 minutes or until tender; drain. When cool, remove pulp, leaving ½-inch shells; coarsely chop pulp and edible seeds.

2. Melt butter in large skillet over medium heat. Brush half of the butter inside chayote shells. Add onion and garlic to remaining butter in skillet; cook until onion is tender. Add tomato and parsley; simmer 5 minutes or until liquid has evaporated. Remove from heat; stir in corn, salt, pepper and chayote pulp.

3. Preheat oven to 375°F. Place chayote shells in greased shallow baking pan. Evenly fill shells with corn mixture; top with cheese. Bake, uncovered, 15 minutes or until chayotes are hot and cheese is melted. *Makes 4 servings*

STUFFED SUMMER SQUASH: Follow directions for Stuffed Chayotes but use 8 large pattypan squash or 8 zucchini (each about 6 inches long) in place of chayotes. Boil whole squash 8 to 10 minutes or until barely tender. After scooping out pulp, turn shells upside down on paper towels to drain before filling. Makes 8 servings.

STUFFED CHAYOTES

THREE BEAN SALAD WITH NOPALITOS

1 can (17 ounces) green lima beans, drained
1 can (15½ ounces) garbanzo beans, drained
1 can (15½ ounces) kidney beans, drained
1 cup canned nopalitos, drained
1 cup thinly sliced celery
¼ cup thinly sliced green onions with tops
½ cup olive oil
3 tablespoons sherry wine vinegar or red wine vinegar
1 teaspoon grated lemon peel
1 teaspoon lemon juice
¾ teaspoon salt
½ teaspoon paprika
¼ teaspoon black pepper
¼ cup chopped fresh parsley

1. Combine beans, nopalitos, celery and green onions in large bowl.

2. Whisk oil, vinegar, lemon peel, lemon juice, salt, paprika and pepper in small bowl until well blended; stir in parsley.

3. Pour over bean mixture; toss gently until vegetables are well coated. Cover; refrigerate 2 hours or overnight for flavors to blend. *Makes 6 to 8 servings*

Mexican Refried Beans

1 can (1 pound 14 ounces) refried beans
1 package (1.0 ounce) LAWRY'S® Taco Spices
    & Seasonings
2 cups (8 ounces) shredded cheddar cheese
¼ cup finely chopped onion

In 2½-quart casserole dish, combine all ingredients. Cover and bake in 350°F oven for 20 to 25 minutes.

Makes about 4 cups (6 to 8 servings)

MEAL IDEA: Serve with your favorite Mexican foods—tacos, burritos, taquitos, flautas, enchiladas and more!

PREP TIME: 10 minutes
COOK TIME: 20 to 25 minutes

Ensalada de Nopalitos (Cactus Salad)

1 jar (16 to 20 ounces) water-packed nopalitos
3 medium tomatoes, blanched, peeled, seeded
    and chopped*
3 tablespoons diced white onion
  Salt
3 tablespoons oil and vinegar salad dressing
1 tablespoon chopped fresh cilantro leaves

*To blanch tomatoes, using a small, sharp knife, cut an "x" in the bottom of each tomato (not the stem end). Briefly plunge the tomatoes into a large pot of boiling water, just long enough to loosen the skins, about 30 seconds. When cool enough to handle, peel the skins. To seed the tomatoes, cut the tomatoes in half crosswise (not lengthwise). Holding a tomato half in the palm of one hand, gently squeeze the seeds out, using the tip of a small knife to scrape out any stubborn seeds.

1. Rinse nopalitos in cold water; drain.

2. Combine nopalitos, tomatoes and onion in serving bowl. Season with salt. Add dressing; toss gently to coat. Garnish with cilantro.

Makes 6 servings

Salads & Sides　141

Festive Finales

MEXICAN WEDDING COOKIES

1 cup pecan pieces or halves
1 cup (2 sticks) butter, softened
2 cups powdered sugar, divided
2 cups all-purpose flour, divided
2 teaspoons vanilla
⅛ teaspoon salt

1. Place pecans in food processor. Process using on/off pulsing action until pecans are ground but not pasty.

2. Beat butter and ½ cup powdered sugar in large bowl at medium speed of electric mixer until light and fluffy. Gradually add 1 cup flour, vanilla and salt. Beat at low speed until well blended. Stir in remaining 1 cup flour and ground nuts with spoon. Shape dough into ball; wrap in plastic wrap and refrigerate 1 hour or until firm.

3. Preheat oven to 350°F. Shape dough into 1-inch balls. Place 1 inch apart on ungreased cookie sheets.

4. Bake 12 to 15 minutes or until golden brown. Let cookies stand on cookie sheets 2 minutes.

5. Meanwhile, place 1 cup powdered sugar in 13×9-inch glass dish. Transfer hot cookies to powdered sugar. Roll cookies in powdered sugar, coating well. Let cookies cool in sugar.

6. Sift remaining ½ cup powdered sugar over sugar-coated cookies before serving. Store tightly covered at room temperature or freeze up to 1 month.

Makes about 4 dozen cookies

MEXICAN WEDDING COOKIES

CARAMEL FLAN

1 cup sugar, divided
2 cups half-and-half
1 cup milk
1½ teaspoons vanilla
6 eggs
2 egg yolks
Fresh whole and sliced strawberries (optional)

1. Preheat oven to 325°F. Heat 5½- to 6-cup ring mold in oven 10 minutes or until hot.

2. Heat ½ cup sugar in heavy, medium skillet over medium-high heat 5 to 8 minutes or until sugar is completely melted and deep amber color, stirring frequently. *Do not allow sugar to burn.*

3. Immediately pour caramelized sugar into ring mold. Holding mold with potholder, quickly rotate to coat bottom and sides evenly with sugar. Place mold on wire rack. *Caution: Caramelized sugar is very hot; do not touch it.*

4. Combine half-and-half and milk in heavy 2-quart saucepan. Heat over medium heat until almost simmering; remove from heat. Add remaining ½ cup sugar and vanilla; stir until sugar is dissolved.

5. Lightly beat eggs and egg yolks in large bowl until blended but not foamy; gradually stir in milk mixture. Pour custard into ring mold.

6. Place mold in large baking pan; pour hot water into baking pan to depth of ½ inch. Bake 35 to 40 minutes or until knife inserted into center of custard comes out clean.

7. Remove mold from water bath; place on wire rack. Let stand 30 minutes. Cover; refrigerate 1½ to 2 hours or until thoroughly chilled.

8. To serve, loosen inner and outer edges of flan with tip of small knife. Cover mold with rimmed serving plate; invert and lift off mold. Garnish with strawberries, if desired. Spoon melted caramel over each serving. *Makes 6 to 8 servings*

CARAMEL FLAN

PECAN PRALINE COOKIES

PRALINE
1½ cups chopped pecans
½ cup granulated sugar
3 tablespoons water

COOKIES
1¼ cups firmly packed light brown sugar
¾ cup Butter Flavor CRISCO® all-vegetable shortening
   or ¾ Butter Flavor CRISCO® stick
2 tablespoons milk
1 tablespoon vanilla
1 egg
1¾ cups all-purpose flour
1 teaspoon salt
¾ teaspoon baking soda

1. Heat oven to 375°F. Place sheets of foil on countertop for cooling cookies.

2. For praline, spread pecans on baking sheet; bake at 375°F for 10 minutes or until lightly toasted, stirring several times. Reserve pecans. Grease baking sheet.

3. Place granulated sugar and water in small saucepan. Bring to boil, stirring occasionally. Cover; boil 2 minutes. Uncover; cook 2 minutes or until mixture becomes golden brown in color. Add reserved pecans; stir until evenly coated. Spread on prepared baking sheet. Cool completely. Place hardened praline in heavy resealable bag; seal. Crush with bottom of small heavy skillet until pieces are small.

4. For cookies, place brown sugar, shortening, milk and vanilla in large bowl. Beat at medium speed of electric mixer until well blended. Add egg; beat well.

5. Combine flour, salt and baking soda. Add to shortening mixture; beat at low speed just until blended. Stir in 1½ cups of crushed praline.

continued on page 148

PECAN PRALINE COOKIES

6. Shape dough into 1-inch balls. Dip top of each ball into remaining crushed praline. Place 3 inches apart on ungreased baking sheets.

7. Bake one baking sheet at a time at 375° for 9 to 11 minutes or cookies are lightly browned. *Do not overbake.* Cool 2 minutes on baking sheet. Remove cookies to foil to cool completely.   ***Makes about 3 dozen cookies***

CINNAMON HONEY ICE CREAM

  2 cups milk
  ¾ cup honey
  1 teaspoon cinnamon
     Pinch salt
  2 eggs, beaten
  2 cups heavy cream
  2 teaspoons vanilla

1. Heat milk in two-quart saucepan over medium heat but do not boil; stir in honey, cinnamon and salt.

2. Pour about ½ cup hot milk into eggs and beat with whisk; pour eggs into saucepan with remaining milk mixture.

3. Cook and stir over medium-low heat 5 minutes (mixture should thicken slightly).

4. Cool to room temperature. Stir in cream and vanilla. Refrigerate overnight or until cold.

5. Freeze in ice cream maker according to manufacturer's directions.   ***Makes 10 to 12 servings***

Mexican Sugar Cookies (Polvorones)

1 cup (2 sticks) butter, softened
½ cup powdered sugar
2 tablespoons milk
1 teaspoon vanilla
1 teaspoon ground cinnamon, divided
1½ to 1¾ cups all-purpose flour
1 teaspoon baking powder
1 cup granulated sugar
1 square (1 ounce) semisweet chocolate, finely grated

1. Preheat oven to 325°F. Grease cookie sheets; set aside.

2. Beat butter, powdered sugar, milk, vanilla and ½ teaspoon cinnamon in large bowl at medium speed of electric mixer until light and fluffy. Gradually add 1½ cups flour and baking powder. Beat at low speed until well blended. Stir in additional flour with spoon if dough is too soft to shape.

3. Shape tablespoonfuls of dough into 1¼-inch balls. Place balls 3 inches apart on prepared cookie sheets. Flatten each ball into 2-inch round with bottom of glass dipped in granulated sugar.

4. Bake 20 to 25 minutes or until edges are golden brown. Let stand on cookie sheets 3 to 4 minutes.

5. Meanwhile, combine granulated sugar, grated chocolate and remaining ½ teaspoon cinnamon in small bowl. Transfer warm cookies, one at a time, to sugar mixture; coat both sides. Remove to wire racks; cool completely.

6. Store tightly covered at room temperature up to 2 weeks or freeze up to 3 months.   *Makes about 2 dozen cookies*

FRUIT TRAY WITH HONEY-LIME SAUCE

1 cantaloupe, seeded and peeled

1 papaya, seeded and peeled

1 small fresh pineapple, peeled, cored and cut into triangles or short spears

1½ cups strawberries, hulled, *or* 6 fresh figs, cut in half

2 kiwifruit, peeled and thinly sliced

1 cup (½ pint) whipping cream

3 tablespoons honey

1 teaspoon grated lime peel

2 teaspoons lime juice

2 bananas, peeled

1 pasteurized egg white*

Mint sprig for garnish

*Use only Grade A, clean, uncracked egg.

1. Cut cantaloupe and papaya into ½-inch crescents. Arrange cantaloupe, papaya, pineapple, strawberries and kiwifruit on large serving platter. Cover and chill up to 4 hours. Whip cream in medium bowl until soft peaks form. Fold in honey, lime peel and lime juice. Cover and refrigerate 2 hours for flavors to blend.

2. To serve, slice bananas crosswise; arrange on fruit platter. Beat egg white in small bowl until stiff peaks form; fold into whipped cream mixture. Spoon into serving bowl; serve with fruit. Garnish with mint.   *Makes about 8 servings*

FRUIT TRAY WITH HONEY-LIME SAUCE

Dulce de Leche

1 (14-ounce) can EAGLE BRAND® Sweetened Condensed Milk (NOT evaporated milk)

Assorted dippers, such as cookies, cake, pound cake, angel food cake cubes, banana chunks, orange slices, apple slices and/or strawberries

1. Preheat oven to 425°F. Pour EAGLE BRAND® into 9-inch pie plate. Cover with foil; place in larger shallow baking pan. Pour hot water into larger pan to depth of 1 inch.

2. Bake 1 hour or until thick and caramel-colored. Beat until smooth. Cool 1 hour. Refrigerate until serving time. Serve as dip with assorted dippers. Store covered in refrigerator for up to 1 week. *Makes about 1¼ cups dip*

CAUTION: Never heat an unopened can.

PREP TIME : 5 minutes
BAKE TIME: 1 hour
COOL TIME: 1 hour

Biscochitos

3 cups all-purpose flour
2 teaspoons anise seeds
1½ teaspoons baking powder
½ teaspoon salt
1 cup (2 sticks) butter
¾ cup sugar, divided
1 egg
¼ cup orange juice
2 teaspoons ground cinnamon

1. Preheat oven to 350°F. Combine flour, anise seeds, baking powder and salt in medium bowl; set aside. Beat butter in large bowl at medium speed of electric mixer until creamy. Add ½ cup sugar; beat until fluffy. Blend in egg. Gradually add flour mixture alternately with orange juice, mixing well after each addition.

2. Divide dough in half. Roll out one portion at a time on lightly floured surface to ¼-inch thickness; cover remaining dough to prevent drying. Cut dough with 2- to 2½-inch cookie cutters. Gather scraps and re-roll. If dough becomes too soft to handle, refrigerate briefly. Place cookies 1 inch apart on ungreased cookie sheets.

3. Combine remaining ¼ cup sugar and cinnamon; lightly sprinkle over cookies. Bake 8 to 10 minutes or until edges are lightly browned. Remove to wire racks; cool completely. Store in airtight container. *Makes 4 to 5 dozen cookies*

Acknowledgments

The publisher would like to thank the companies and organizations
listed below for the use of their recipes and photographs
in this publication.

American Lamb Council

Bob Evans®

Butterball® Turkey

Chef Paul Prudhomme's Magic Seasoning Blends®

Crisco is a registered trademark of The J.M. Smucker Company

Del Monte Corporation

Dole Food Company, Inc.

Eagle Brand® Sweetened Condensed Milk

The Golden Grain Company®

Heinz North America

The Hidden Valley® Food Products Company

Hormel Foods, LLC

Jennie-O Turkey Store®

Lawry's® Foods

MASTERFOODS USA

National Chicken Council / US Poultry & Egg Association

National Pork Board

Newman's Own, Inc.®

Ortega®, A Division of B&G Foods, Inc.

Reckitt Benckiser Inc.

Sargento® Foods Inc.

Unilever Foods North America

Wisconsin Milk Marketing Board

Index 157

Notes

METRIC CONVERSION CHART

VOLUME MEASUREMENTS (dry)

1/8 teaspoon = 0.5 mL
1/4 teaspoon = 1 mL
1/2 teaspoon = 2 mL
3/4 teaspoon = 4 mL
1 teaspoon = 5 mL
1 tablespoon = 15 mL
2 tablespoons = 30 mL
1/4 cup = 60 mL
1/3 cup = 75 mL
1/2 cup = 125 mL
2/3 cup = 150 mL
3/4 cup = 175 mL
1 cup = 250 mL
2 cups = 1 pint = 500 mL
3 cups = 750 mL
4 cups = 1 quart = 1 L

VOLUME MEASUREMENTS (fluid)

1 fluid ounce (2 tablespoons) = 30 mL
4 fluid ounces (1/2 cup) = 125 mL
8 fluid ounces (1 cup) = 250 mL
12 fluid ounces (1 1/2 cups) = 375 mL
16 fluid ounces (2 cups) = 500 mL

WEIGHTS (mass)

1/2 ounce = 15 g
1 ounce = 30 g
3 ounces = 90 g
4 ounces = 120 g
8 ounces = 225 g
10 ounces = 285 g
12 ounces = 360 g
16 ounces = 1 pound = 450 g

DIMENSIONS

1/16 inch = 2 mm
1/8 inch = 3 mm
1/4 inch = 6 mm
1/2 inch = 1.5 cm
3/4 inch = 2 cm
1 inch = 2.5 cm

OVEN TEMPERATURES

250°F = 120°C
275°F = 140°C
300°F = 150°C
325°F = 160°C
350°F = 180°C
375°F = 190°C
400°F = 200°C
425°F = 220°C
450°F = 230°C

BAKING PAN SIZES

Utensil	Size in Inches/Quarts	Metric Volume	Size in Centimeters
Baking or Cake Pan (square or rectangular)	8×8×2	2 L	20×20×5
	9×9×2	2.5 L	23×23×5
	12×8×2	3 L	30×20×5
	13×9×2	3.5 L	33×23×5
Loaf Pan	8×4×3	1.5 L	20×10×7
	9×5×3	2 L	23×13×7
Round Layer Cake Pan	8×1½	1.2 L	20×4
	9×1½	1.5 L	23×4
Pie Plate	8×1¼	750 mL	20×3
	9×1¼	1 L	23×3
Baking Dish or Casserole	1 quart	1 L	—
	1½ quart	1.5 L	—
	2 quart	2 L	—